Sunset Scandinavian Cook Book

By the Editors of Sunset Books and Sunset Magazine

Lane Publishing Co., Menlo Park, California

Acknowledgments
We wish to express our sincere appreciation for assistance in preparing this book to: Lars Malmstrom, Swedish Information Service, San Francisco; Ingrid Ekestrom and Sverker Abrahamsson, *Hem-O-Fritid,* and Astrid Rejnholm, *Allt Om Mat,* Stockholm; Charlotte and Bengt Reimersson, Vasteras, Sweden; Goran Hoving, Finnish National Tourist Office, New York City; Helena Vuorenjuuri, *Anna,* Helsinki; Per Holte, Scandinavian National Tourist Offices, Los Angeles.

Edited by Jerry Anne Di Vecchio

Coordinating Editor: Judith A. Gaulke

Design: JoAnn Masaoka

Illustrations: Mark Gobe

Front Cover: Photograph by Glenn Christiansen
Design Consultant: William Cheney

Back Cover Photographs: Top left: Karen Hammond.
Top right: Gordon Hammond.
Top center, bottom right: Glenn Christiansen.
Bottom left: Darrow M. Watt.

Photographers: Glenn Christiansen: pages 4, 17, 55, 68, 76, 78.
Norman A. Plate: pages 16, 20.
Darrow M. Watt: pages 8, 11, 13, 15, 36, 42, 52.

Executive Editor, Sunset Books: David E. Clark

Contents

Special Features

Scandinavian Food Discoveries

Tasting the delights of Norway, Sweden, Denmark, and Finland

Scandinavia has long been renowned for its long summer days and winter nights. But the foods served during those long days and nights in Norway, Sweden, Denmark, and Finland are equally worthy of renown. Such Scandinavian contributions to world cuisine as open-faced sandwiches and sumptuous buffets surely qualify these countries for the gastronomic respect of cooks everywhere.

Scandinavia is a land of oceans, seas, penetrating fjords, thousands of lakes, islands, flat land, and dramatic mountains. Its climate varies from the warmth of summer—when Scandinavians spill joyously, almost religiously, out into the sun—to the chill of classically rigorous winters. How Scandinavians eat and what they eat has evolved logically from these natural influences.

This book is a summary of the discoveries of Sunset editors in Scandinavia, including dishes old and new. Additionally, the book reflects the extensive Scandinavian influence in the United States. Many a good cook directly from Scandinavia, or perhaps living a generation or two in this country, has shared treasured family recipes with us, and we have thoroughly tested all of them in Sunset's kitchens. You will find dishes, menus, and party plans of a practical but refreshing nature for constant use.

Country-style smörgåsbord: *a great way to entertain, described on page 28. All the foods can be prepared ahead or purchased; you serve yourself in courses.*

Sandwiches

Scandinavian Ingenuity at the "bread-and-butter table"

Copenhagen is on the island of Zealand, so if you're going there, you travel by boat. Once on board, there's nothing to do but eat. The boat serves a buffet that Scandinavians casually call a bread-and-butter table (the "smör" of *smörgåsbord* means butter) but which is the most copious, varied, and delicious buffet anyone is ever likely to encounter.

Always served are many kinds of good bread, soft or crunchy, and quantities of butter. And to go with it, expect a meal such as Odin must have invented for the hungry warriors of Valhalla: herring in a dozen forms, salmon, caviar, cheeses, and thin-sliced meats. If you sail at dinner time, this is just an introduction, a snack. The real meal follows.

The chapter that follows describes how to prepare at home the lighter elements of such a buffet table. Included are the sandwiches and their many accompaniments and the Finnish sandwich pastries. Try them at any time of day—for breakfast, lunch, or dinner, for a snack or a meal. And don't be surprised when they impress your guests. In later chapters you'll find some of the hot dishes and salads that may also be served at a Scandinavian feast, creating an even more impressive version of the *smörgåsbord*.

The Smørrebrød Idea

Strolling down a Copenhagen street, a traveller is likely to come upon a vending machine that is selling—not gumballs, newspapers, or candy—but open-faced sandwiches. This is *smørrebrød*, a word that has the root meaning of buttered bread but has now come to mean a collection of edibles on a slice of bread arranged with such attention to form and color that the eye feasts before the palate.

There are restaurants that specialize in this edible art form, offering dozens of kinds from which to choose, but the choice is made less difficult by the custom of eating several kinds at a sitting.

Try your own copies of these sandwiches for breakfast, lunch, or dinner. You can use them and the special foods served with them for any occasion from a snack to a dinner party.

A Whole-Tray-at-Once of Sandwiches

Separate 12 to 15 slices Westphalian-style **pumpernickel bread** and spread thickly with **sour cream** or cream cheese (you'll need ¾ to 1 cup). Top 4 or 5 slices evenly with about 1 cup (¼ lb.) tiny, whole, cooked and shelled **shrimp** and about 3 tablespoons chopped **green onions** (including some tops). Arrange on *each* of 4 or 5 more slices of the bread 4 slices of **pickled beets** and 4 small pieces **prepared herring.** Cover the remaining slices of bread with sliced **radishes** (10 or 12) and sprinkle with **salt** and dried **dill weed,** or chopped fresh dill. Cut each sandwich in quarters. Makes 12 appetizer servings or 48 to 60 portions.

Anchovy and Onion

Butter thin slices of firm **white bread** and cut into 3 to 4-inch squares or rectangles, removing crusts. Top each with a mound of chopped **green onions** (including some tops), 2 canned, flat **anchovy fillets,** crossed, and a small spoonful of sieved, hard-cooked **egg yolk.**

Beef Caviar Loaf

Cut 2 long horizontal slices, *each* about ½ inch thick, from the center of a loaf (about 1 lb.) of **French bread.** Toast on both sides under broiler. Cool, then spread with **butter.**

Thinly slice about a 1-pound piece of fat-trimmed, cold, rare **beef steak** or roast. Evenly divide slices and arrange half the meat on each buttered toast slice; **salt** meat very lightly.

Spoon a band of black **caviar** (from sturgeon or other fish) down the center of the beef, allowing 1 to 2 tablespoons for each toast slice. Garnish with a few slivers of **green onion** tops or sprigs of fresh dill and serve with green onions. Cut in sections to serve. Makes 8 to 10 portions.

Beef with Caviar

Butter 4 slices of **rye bread.** Cover each piece of buttered bread with overlapping thin slices of cold rare **beef steak** or roast (about 8 oz. for 4 sandwiches). On each, place a spoonful of **sour cream** in one corner and a spoonful of **caviar** (from sturgeon or other fish) next to it. Garnish with a few finely chopped **green onions.** Makes 4 sandwiches.

Beef with Horseradish Cream

Follow directions for Beef with Caviar sandwich, omitting the caviar. Blend ¼ cup **sour cream** with 1 teaspoon **prepared horseradish;** then spoon onto sandwiches. Top each with 1 or 2 tablespoons **Danish Crisp Onions** (see page 45).

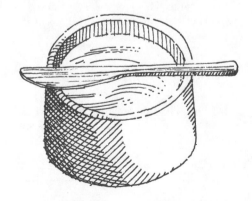

Caviar: How to Buy... How to Make

Red-gold salmon *caviar, a homemade treat.*

Glistening mounds of caviar add a special glamour to foods.

You can choose the preserved dark caviars (prepared eggs or roe) of sturgeon, lumpfish, or whitefish; fresh and perishable sturgeon caviar; or preserved red caviar from salmon. Lumpfish and whitefish caviars are dyed to simulate the natural gray to black hues of sturgeon caviar. The name of the fish is always on the label, except for sturgeon caviar, which may be labeled just caviar.

Price is no guide to how caviar is enjoyed. The cost range may be from just a few cents to many dollars for each ounce; yet even caviar connoisseurs find that caviars made from fish roes other than sturgeon are very good and certainly more practical.

Each caviar does have unique qualities. You might keep in mind that fresh sturgeon caviar is usually salted more lightly than all others; preserved sturgeon caviar is more liquid in consistency; lumpfish caviar has an interesting, crunchy texture; whitefish caviar is tiny and tender; preserved salmon caviar is the most pungent.

To reduce the saltiness of the less costly caviars, you can rinse them in a wire strainer under cool running water, drain well, and then chill before serving. This process also removes any excess coloring that may stain foods decorated by the caviar.

Making Fresh Red Caviar

During late summer and on into the fall when salmon spawn, the time is right to obtain fresh salmon roe from a fisherman friend or purchase it at a fish market (you will probably have to place an order at a market and wait a few days).

Preparing the roe (eggs) is simple, and the result is a delicate caviar with a lightly salted sea flavor. Near maturity, the roe will be large and well shaped, and will separate readily from the skein (a membrane that binds the eggs together).

A heavy, oily aroma is naturally present in the membrane of the roe; clean within 24 hours of purchase (discard if there is any odor of spoilage). The prepared eggs have a light fragrance.

If the skeins have been frozen, the eggs are much more fragile and the membrane is harder to remove; the caviar, though, will taste fine.

Prepared salmon caviar will keep, tightly covered, in the refrigerator for several months.

With your fingers, gently pop the eggs individually from the skein; the more membrane you remove at this point, the easier the task becomes later. A ½-pound skein (typical size from a 12 to 14-lb. fish) will yield 1 to 1½ cups of eggs, depending upon your dexterity, patience, and the maturity of the eggs.

For *each* 1 to 2 cups of cleaned salmon eggs, stir ½ cup of salt with 2 cups of cold water in a large bowl until the salt is mostly dissolved. Pour in the eggs and swirl them about briefly; then let stand 30 minutes to firm. Pick out floating particles of white membrane.

Drain the caviar; then dump it into a large bowl of cold water, swirling gently to rinse; then drain again. Pick out remaining membrane. Chill, covered, before serving. Keep tightly covered and refrigerated up to several months or as long as the flavor is pleasant. Serve on plain, unsalted wafers or toast or bread spread with sweet butter or a dollop of sour cream (mixed, perhaps, with chopped chives or green onions).

Blue Cheese with Cherries

Butter 3-inch squares of thinly sliced **rye bread** (crusts removed). Top each with a slice of **blue cheese** (about 2 oz. for 6 sandwiches) and a small spoonful of **cherry preserves**.

Cream Cheese with Apricots

Generously spread round **butter puff wafers** with soft **cream cheese** (two small 3 oz. packages for 6 sandwiches). Top each with a fresh or **dried apricot** half, a **walnut** half, and a small spoonful of red **currant jelly**.

Egg Salad on Tomato Slice

Arrange leaves of **butter lettuce** on each of 6 small round slices of **buttered,** buffet-style **rye bread.** Top each with a thin **tomato** slice and equal portions of this mixture: mash 2 hard-cooked **eggs** and blend with ¼ cup finely chopped **celery,** 4 teaspoons **mayonnaise,** ¼ teaspoon **dry mustard,** and **salt** and **pepper** to taste. Garnish with **dill** or parsley sprigs, or clusters of cress or alfalfa sprouts. Makes 6 sandwiches.

Gouda with Grapes

To make each sandwich, arrange leaves of **butter lettuce** on **buttered rye melba toast.** Cover with a thin slice of **Gouda cheese** and top with 1 or 2 **grape** halves.

Ham and Cheese with Spiced Peach

For each sandwich, **butter** a thin slice of **rye bread.** Top each slice with a large leaf of **butter lettuce** and lay 2 or 3 thin slices of **Tybo cheese** or other mild cheese on the lettuce. Roll up 1 or 2 thin slices of cooked **ham** and set on the side of the sandwich. Drain canned **spiced peaches;** put one beside the ham on each sandwich. Garnish with a sprig of **watercress,** a cluster of cress or alfalfa sprouts.

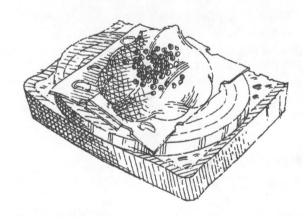

Liverwurst and Onions with Caviar

To make each sandwich, top a slice of Westphalian-style **pumpernickel bread** with a thin slice of large, mild **onion;** then cover with 2 thin slices of **liverwurst.** Top with 2 or 3 teaspoons of **sour cream,** then a portion of black caviar (from sturgeon or other fish) blended with onion (allow 3 tablespoons **caviar** mixed with 2 tablespoons minced **onion** for 6 to 8 sandwiches). Sprinkle sandwiches lightly with dried **dill weed,** chopped fresh dill, or garnish with a dill sprig.

Opera Sandwich

For each serving, top a thick slice of toasted and **buttered French bread** with a broiled **ground beef** patty (preferably rare); then set a softly fried **egg** on the meat. Season with **salt** and **pepper.** Garnish on the side with **butter lettuce** leaf, sprigs of dill, or a cluster of alfalfa sprouts, and a **tomato** slice.

Petit Beef Tartar

Mix thoroughly ½ pound of **ground beef sirloin,** ¼ teaspoon **garlic salt,** ¼ teaspoon **tarragon leaves** (optional), ⅛ teaspoon **seasoned pepper;** add **salt** to taste. Cut about 3 large **onions** in ¼-inch-thick slices; separate about 3 dozen of the inner, bite-sized rings, reserving the rest for other uses.

Place small onion rings side by side on a serving tray; nest in each ring about 1 teaspoon of the beef. Cover and chill until ready to serve.

(Continued on next page)

Crack 1 **egg** (reserve white for another use) and put the yolk in a shell half; set this shell in an onion ring on the beef tray. Accompany with 8 or 9 slices of **buttered,** Westphalian-style **pumpernickel bread,** cut into quarters. Lift a portion of onion and beef onto the bread; spoon on a little of the egg yolk. Makes about 36 portions.

Pickled Herring and Egg Yolk

Butter 4 thin slices of **pumpernickel bread** generously, top each slice with **lettuce** leaf, place **onion** ring (about 1¼ inch diameter) in one corner, and surround with drained, **prepared herring** tidbits (about 12 oz. for 4 sandwiches). Just before serving, slip a raw **egg yolk** into each onion ring. Garnish, if desired, with a cluster of **alfalfa** or cress **sprouts.** Makes 4 sandwiches.

Salmon and Cucumber

Combine small package (3 oz.) **cream cheese** with 1 teaspoon **lemon juice;** spread on 2 slices of **pumpernickel bread.** Arrange about 6 **cucumber** slices on each sandwich and top with thinly sliced and rolled *gravlax* (see page 14) or sliced, rolled, lightly smoked salmon (allow about 3 oz. of either), or 1 can (about 3½ oz.) sliced or chunk-style smoked salmon. Garnish with chopped **green onion,** chopped chives, or a cluster of **alfalfa** or cress **sprouts.** Makes 2 sandwiches.

A Smørrebrød Buffet for Six

Here is a handsome and colorful meal, perfect for holiday parties or a summer buffet. You can make these sandwiches up to 3 hours before serving, arrange them on trays, cover with clear plastic wrap, and chill.

It may take one person as long as 2 hours to prepare the sandwiches after all the ingredients are assembled.

First Course

Dilled Green Pea Soup (see page 19)
Choice of: Salmon and Cucumber (see page 10)
      Anchovy and Onion (see page 7)
      Shrimp and Asparagus (see page 11)
      Egg Salad on Tomato (see page 9)

Main Course

Choice of: Turkey Breast with Red Cabbage (see page 11)
      Beef with Horseradish Cream (see page 7)
      Ham and Cheese with Spiced Peach (see page 9)

Dessert

Choice of: Blue Cheese with Cherries (see page 9)
      Cream Cheese with Apricots (see page 9)
      Tybo Cheese with Marmalade (see page 11)
      Gouda with Grapes (see page 9)
      Beer   Aquavit   Coffee

Before guests arrive, arrange a buffet table with soup cups or mugs and two sets of sandwich plates (one for the first course, one for the main course). Have bottled beer and aquavit in ice. Also set individual places at small tables with knives, forks, napkins, glasses for beer and aquavit, and coffee cups. At serving time, bring the first course and main dish *smørrebrød* to the buffet table with hot soup; your guests serve themselves to these two courses. Later, replace sandwich plates with small dessert plates and pass dessert *smørrebrød* selection with hot coffee.

Make the soup ahead and reheat just before serving. Allow two or three *smørrebrød* at each course for each guest; offer a variety of two to four kinds at each course from the list above or from among the other sandwiches described in this chapter.

Salmon with Egg

Cut 4 thin center slices from 2 hard-cooked **eggs** and reserve. Mash remaining egg with 2 table-spoons **mayonnaise.** Spread egg mixture on 2 slices plain or **buttered whole wheat bread.** Top with thin slices of *gravlax* (see page 14), or lightly smoked salmon (about ⅛ lb. of either), or 1 can (about 7 oz.) salmon, drained. Garnish with **egg** slices and sprigs of **watercress,** or dill sprigs. Makes 2 sandwiches.

Shrimp and Asparagus

Cut thin slices of firm **white bread** into 2 by 4-inch rectangles, removing crusts. Spread with **butter** or margarine. Top each with a lengthwise row of tiny, whole, cooked and shelled **shrimp** (about 2 oz. for 6 sandwiches) and spear of cold, cooked (or canned) **asparagus,** cut to fit bread. Spoon a dollop of curry-seasoned mayonnaise (¼ teaspoon **curry powder** blended with each 1 tablespoon **mayonnaise**) on the edge of the sandwich.

Turkey Breast with Red Cabbage

Butter thin slices of firm **white bread.** Top each with overlapping thin slices of cooked **turkey breast** (about ½ lb. for 6 sandwiches). At one corner of each sandwich, place 1 small leaf of **butter lettuce.** Fill with 1 or 2 tablespoons well drained, canned **sweet-sour red cabbage** and top with ½ to 1 tablespoon of **sour cream** and 1 piece of **spiced watermelon rind.**

Tybo Cheese with Marmalade

Butter crisp, rectangular **tea biscuits.** Top each with 2 thin slices **Tybo cheese** or other mild cheese (about 2 oz. for 6 sandwiches) and a spoon-ful of **orange marmalade;** garnish with a **citrus blossom** or a thin slice of lemon.

Sandwich Loaf Cake

Three fillings and eight layers of dark and light bread go into this sandwich loaf. It's impressive

Multi-layer sandwich loaf *with three kinds of fillings; slice and serve for party luncheon entrée.*

on a buffet table, or you can serve it with salad and dessert for a simple meal.

Have the bakery cut two loaves of bread, one dark, one light, in lengthwise slices about ½ inch thick. The night before, make the fillings and, if you wish, assemble the sandwich loaf layers then, too. Cover with clear plastic film and chill. Then, several hours before serving, frost and garnish the exterior of the loaf.

1 rectangular, sandwich-style loaf
    dark bread (wheat or rye, about 1
    lb.), sliced lengthwise
1 rectangular sandwich-style loaf
    white bread (about 1 lb.), sliced
    lengthwise
½ cup (¼ lb.) soft butter or margarine
    Avocado Filling (recipe follows)
    Deviled Ham Filling (recipe follows)
    Liverwurst Filling (recipe follows)
    Parsley Cheese Spread (recipe
     follows)
    Thin slices cucumber
    Parsley sprigs or chopped parsley

Remove top and bottom crust slices of both loaves. Trim 8 dark slices and 8 white slices to exactly 3 by 6 inches, cutting away crust. Reserve remaining bread for other uses.

To assemble the sandwich loaf, place 2 slices of white bread side by side on a flat serving plate (they should make a square). Spread with soft butter or margarine, then with ⅓ of the Avocado Filling.

Place 2 slices of dark bread side by side on the filling, laying them at right angles to the white bread slices (edges should be even). Spread with butter or margarine, then with about ⅓ of the Deviled Ham Filling.

Place 2 slices of white bread side by side over filling to make the third layer at right angles to the dark slices. Spread with butter or margarine, then with about ½ of the Liverwurst Filling.

Repeat layering, spreading the fourth layer with another ⅓ of the Avocado Filling, the fifth with ⅓ of the Deviled Ham Filling, the sixth with the rest of the Liverwurst Filling, the seventh with the rest of the Avocado Filling. Place the remaining slices on top. You can do this much ahead of time; cover with clear plastic film and refrigerate as long as overnight.

Spread the top of the loaf with the last of the Deviled Ham Filling and frost the sides with Parsley Cheese Spread. Garnish the top of the loaf with thin slices of cucumber and sprigs of parsley (or chopped parsley). Refrigerate, covered, at least 2 hours or until serving time. With a sharp knife, cut in vertical slices to serve. Makes 8 main dish or 16 appetizer servings.

Avocado Filling. Mash 1 large ripe **avocado** with 3 tablespoons **lemon juice,** 1 small package (3 oz.) soft **cream cheese,** and ¼ teaspoon **salt,** creaming together until smooth. Makes about 1¼ cups.

Deviled Ham Filling. Mix together 2 cans (4½ oz. each) **deviled ham,** 2 tablespoons minced **onion,** ¼ teaspoon **pepper,** ½ teaspoon **prepared hot mustard,** and 2 tablespoons soft **butter** or margarine. Makes about 1¼ cups.

Liverwurst Filling. Mash ½ pound **liverwurst** and stir in 6 slices cooked and crumbled **bacon,** 1 tablespoon **dry Sherry** or lemon juice, ½ teaspoon dried **dill weed** (or 1½ teaspoons chopped fresh dill) and 2 tablespoons soft **butter** or margarine. Makes about 1¼ cups.

Parsley-Cheese Spread. Smoothly mix 1 large package (8 oz.) **cream cheese** with ¼ cup **whipping cream,** ½ teaspoon **salt,** and 1 cup minced **parsley.** Makes about 1½ cups.

Herring with Bread

Preserved herring, salted or smoked, has been a staple food in Scandinavia since the Middle Ages and before. No self-respecting *smörgåsbord* is complete without at least two or three kinds of prepared herring. A simple meal might consist of nothing but bread and herring; and herring can lead off an elegant banquet.

Herring fanciers will argue a good case for preparing herring dishes with the indisputably smelly Atlantic (or salt) herring packed in a salt brine; these fish are sold whole (with or without heads) in fish markets or delicatessens and require several days to prepare (although the time you spend each day is brief). However, if you are in a hurry or only need a small quantity of herring, you can use the short-cut method of blending some of the more simply-seasoned canned or refrigerated prepared herring with the desired flavoring—or you can make up a supply of herring-from-scratch ahead of time, adding on flavors later.

Each of the following dishes offers alternative methods based on short or long preparation.

Inlagd Sill

(*Pickled Herring*)

Refresh 3 **Atlantic herring** (about 2 lbs. with heads, 1½ lbs. without) in this fashion:

Remove and discard heads (if attached) and empty body cavities. Rinse the herring under cool, running water; then place it in a large bowl of cold water. Cover and chill overnight. The next day, fillet the herring by running a small, sharp knife along the backbone and body cavity to free the fish; do not remove skin. Trim the bottom edge of each fillet to remove fins; cut away the top fin.

To cut the fish for *Inlagd Sill,* slice fillets crosswise in about ½-inch-wide strips.

Peel and thinly slice 2 medium-sized **onions** (preferably red). Also mix together ¼ cup **sugar** and 5 teaspoons **ground allspice.**

In a wide-mouth glass jar (about 5 cups), make a layer of the small tail pieces. Then add alternate layers of herring (silver side placed against the outside of the jar when possible), onions, and sugar mixture until all is used. Pour in enough **white wine vinegar** or cider vinegar (about 2 cups) to cover fish. Cover and chill at least 2 days before serving; store as long as 6 months. After several months' storage, the herring becomes softer and the spice flavor gradually grows more pronounced. Serve, if desired, with bread and butter. Makes 4 to 4½ cups.

Quick Pickled Herring

Drain liquid from 1½ to 2 cups (or 2 jars, *each* 6 to 8 oz.) lightly seasoned, **prepared herring,** such as marinated fat herring fillet pieces or wine-flavored herring fillet pieces. Also peel and thinly slice 1 **carrot** and 1 small **red onion.**

Alternate layers of herring, carrot, onion, and 1 teaspoon **whole allspice** (slightly crushed) in a glass jar or deep container of at least 4-cup capacity until all ingredients are used. Mix together ⅓ cup **white vinegar,** white wine vinegar, or cider vinegar, 1 cup **water,** ⅔ cup **sugar;** pour over herring. Tuck 1 **whole bay leaf** into jar. Cover and chill at least 4 hours or up to 4 days. Serve, if desired, with bread and butter. Makes about 3 cups.

Glazier's Herring

(*Glasmästarsill*)

Drain liquid from 1½ to 2 cups **Inlagd Sill** (see page 12) or lightly seasoned, prepared herring, such as marinated fat herring fillet pieces or wine-flavored herring fillet pieces (2 jars, 6 to 8 oz. *each*). Also peel and dice 1 **carrot** and thinly slice 1 **leek** (white part only) and 1 small **white onion.**

Mix herring with carrot, leek, onion, 1 tablespoon **prepared horseradish,** 1 **whole bay leaf,** 6 to 8 **whole black peppers** (slightly crushed), ⅓ cup *each* **sugar,** and **white vinegar,** white wine vinegar, or cider vinegar, and ⅔ cup **water.** Cover and chill at least 4 hours or up to 4 to 5 days. Serve, if desired, with bread and butter. Makes about 3½ cups.

Curried Herring

Drain liquid from 1½ to 2 cups **Inlagd Sill** (see page 12), or lightly seasoned, prepared herring, such as marinated snack tid-bits, marinated fat herring fillet pieces, or wine-flavored herring fillet pieces (2 jars, 6 to 8 oz. *each*). Blend herring with ¾ cup **mayonnaise,** 1 teaspoon **curry powder,** ¼ teaspoon **ground turmeric,** ⅛ teaspoon **ground coriander,** and a dash of **ground cinnamon.** Cover and chill at least 2 hours or as long as 4 or 5 days before serving. Serve, if desired, with bread and butter. Makes 1½ to 2 cups.

Fillet Atlantic herring *by cutting flesh away from the backbone; use a small sharp knife for the job.*

Alternate layers *of silvery skinned herring pieces and sliced red onion in a jar to make pickled herring.*

Herring in Sour Cream with Apple and Onion

Drain liquid from 1½ to 2 cups *Inlagd Sill* (see page 12), or lightly seasoned, prepared herring, such as marinated snack tid-bits, marinated fat herring fillet pieces, or wine-flavored herring fillet pieces. Blend with 1 medium-sized **red onion,** thinly sliced and separated into rings, 1 large **Newtown Pippin Apple** (or other tart, crisp apple), peeled and finely diced, and 2 cups **sour cream.** Cover and chill at least 2 hours or as long as 4 or 5 days before serving. Garnish with chopped **green onions** (including some tops). Squeeze **lemon juice** onto individual portions, as desired. If you like, accompany with bread and butter. Makes about 4½ cups.

Herring with Tomato Mustard Sauce

In a small saucepan, combine ¾ cup tomato-based **chile sauce,** ½ teaspoon **mustard seed,** ¼ **lemon** (including peel), thinly sliced, and ½ teaspoon **prepared horseradish.** Bring to a boil, stirring. Remove from heat and blend with 1½ to 2 cups drained *Inlagd Sill* (see page 12), or lightly seasoned, prepared herring, such as spiced cut herring, marinated snack tid-bits, marinated fat herring fillet pieces, or wine-flavored herring fillet pieces (2 jars, about 6 to 8 oz. *each*). Cover and chill as long as 4 hours or up to 4 to 5 days before serving. Serve, if desired, with bread and butter. Makes about 2 cups.

Herring with Dill and Juniper

Unroll herring from 1 jar (12 to 13 oz.) refrigerated **herring rollmops.** If necessary, cut herring in half lengthwise to separate fillets. Mix liquid and any seasonings with 10 **whole juniper berries,** crushed slightly (or 2 tablespoons gin), and ¼ teaspoon dried **dill weed** (or ¾ teaspoons chopped fresh dill). Pour liquid over herring. Cover and chill at least overnight or up to 4 days. Sprinkle with a little more dried dill weed or top with dill sprigs to serve. If you like, accompany with bread and butter. Makes about 1 cup.

Baked Smoked Herring

Lift fillets from 2 cans (7 or 8 oz. *each*) **smoked** (kippered) **herring** fillets and place in a shallow baking dish (about 1-qt. size). Discard juices. Moisten surface of herring with 5 tablespoons **whipping cream.** Bake, uncovered, in a 350° oven for 25 to 30 minutes or until bubbling; baste herring occasionally with some of the cream. Serve hot. Accompany with bread and butter. Makes about 2 cups.

Gravlax: Salmon for Sandwiches

The Swedes get credit for this treatment of salmon—very popular throughout Scandinavia—that resembles lightly smoked salmon or kosher-style lox.

Basically, a fresh piece of salmon is coated with a mixture of salt, sugar, and dill. The fish gives up moisture, becoming firm, and changes to a rich red-gold color. Sometimes a weight is placed on the salmon to compress the flesh so it will slice more readily into thin slivers; this step is particularly typical in older recipes. The procedure takes 24 to 48 hours; no cooking is involved.

Mild Gravlax with Sweet Mustard Sauce

A mustard sauce accompanies this version of the salmon; more sugar in the cure gives it a richer taste.

Follow the procedure for making **Piquant** *Grav-lax* (see next page), using a 2-pound, center-section **salmon** fillet with skin removed. Mix the 1 tablespoon finely chopped fresh **dill** or 1 teaspoon dried dill weed with only 2 tablespoons **salt,** increasing **sugar** to ¼ cup. Add 12 **whole black peppers** and omit ground pepper, allspice, and vinegar. Rub mixture onto fish. Cover and chill as directed (omit weight); you can serve after 24 hours. Slice thinly

Salmon, *"cooked" without heat, becomes elegant* gravlax. *It's an ideal picnic main dish or a fine first course.*

across the grain; spoon Sweet Mustard Sauce (directions follow) onto portions as desired. Accompany with hot **buttered white bread toast.** Makes 4 to 6 main dish servings or 8 to 12 first course servings.

Sweet Mustard Sauce. Stir together 2 tablespoons **Swedish mustard** or Dijon mustard, 1 tablespoon **sugar,** 1½ tablespoons **wine vinegar,** ½ teaspoon **salt,** and 1 teaspoon finely chopped fresh **dill** (or ¼ teaspoon dried dill weed). With a fork, gradually and smoothly beat in ⅓ cup **salad oil.** Makes about ⅔ cup.

Piquant Gravlax

Serve thin slices of *gravlax* alone or on bread and butter as a first course, or as a main dish, accompanied by hot boiled potatoes and a vegetable, such as creamed spinach. Or serve it with a potato or macaroni salad, hard-cooked eggs, and sliced tomatoes, perhaps, on a picnic.

  1 teaspoon *each* dried dill weed and
       dill seed (or 1 tablespoon finely
       chopped fresh dill)
    2-pound salmon fillet with skin (can
       be 1 or 2 pieces from a center or
       tail section)
  3 tablespoons salt
  4 teaspoons sugar
  ¼ teaspoon *each* freshly ground black
       pepper and ground allspice
  ¼ cup red or white wine vinegar
       Sour cream (optional)

Mix dill weed and seed (or use just the fresh dill) and sprinkle half in the bottom of a flat dish (such as a glass casserole) that the salmon fits into compactly. Set salmon skin side down in dish; sprinkle with remaining dill. Blend salt, sugar, pepper, and allspice, distributing evenly over salmon and patting onto flesh. Pour vinegar over fish.

Cover dish with clear plastic film and set a weight on the fish—such as a plate holding a pound or so of butter or a large bottle of juice. Refrigerate at least 2 days; spoon juices over fish occasionally during this time. After a day, remove the weights. The salmon keeps as long as a week in the brine but gradually grows too salty to be enjoyable.

Slice fish thinly across the grain on a diagonal to the skin; cut away from skin. Accompany with sour cream. Makes 4 to 6 main dish servings or 8 to 12 first course servings.

Oil-preserved Gravlax

You can keep prepared *gravlax* longer if you use this technique. The oil adds a new and interesting quality to the fish.

Slice freshly prepared ***gravlax*** thinly across the grain. Pack slices into a glass jar or jars; pour in **olive oil** to cover. Slip the tip of a knife between the jar and the salmon to release any trapped air bubbles; then add more oil as necessary to again cover fish. Cover and refrigerate for as long as 2 weeks. Drain briefly on paper towels before serving.

Finnish Sandwich Pastries

(*Piirakka*)

Wholesome treats for breakfast, lunch, or snacking are the Finnish filled rye pastries known as *piirakka* (pi-rahk-kah). Even though *piirakka* with their attractive, oval shape, are considered an old-fashioned country-style dish in Finland, they are very popular. The Finns like them hot or cold, but chances are you'll like them best hot, topped with the spread of butter blended with mashed, hard-cooked egg.

Serve the pastries as you would a sandwich or starchy vegetable to accompany soup, cold meats, cheeses, or salads. Or, like the Finns, you might enjoy them with cool glasses of milk or buttermilk.

    1 cup rye flour
       About ⅓ cup all-purpose flour,
         unsifted
    ¼ teaspoon salt
    6 tablespoons butter or margarine,
         melted and cooled
    1 egg
    ⅓ cup sour cream
       Rice Filling, or Carrot or Cabbage
         Filling (directions follow)
       Egg Butter (directions follow)

In a bowl, stir together rye flour, ⅓ cup all-purpose flour, and salt. Add butter, egg, and sour cream and stir with a fork until well mixed. With lightly floured hands, shape soft dough into a compact ball; then knead on a board lightly coated with all-purpose flour until smooth and easy to handle (takes 2 to 3 minutes). Divide dough into 24 equal pieces, rolling each into a smooth ball. Cover with plastic film to prevent drying.

Shape pastries one at a time. Roll a portion of dough into a circle about 4½ inches in diameter on a board or pastry cloth dusted evenly with all-purpose flour. Spoon 2 tablespoons of the filling onto center of dough, spreading to within ½ to ¾ inch of rim.

Fold opposing rims of the circle over the filling, creating an oval with the filling exposed in the center. With your fingers, pinch the edge of dough alongside the filling.

When all pastries are formed, place slightly apart on a greased baking sheet. Bake in a 350° oven for about 35 minutes or until well browned. Serve hot or warm. If made ahead, cool on wire racks; then cover and chill (or freeze). To reheat, place uncovered on a baking sheet in a 350° oven for 8 to 10 minutes (20 minutes if frozen). As you eat pastries—either out of hand or with a fork—spread with Egg Butter. Makes 24.

Rice Filling. Combine ½ cup **long grain white rice,** ½ teaspoon **salt,** and 3 cups **milk** in the top of a double boiler. Place over simmering water, cover, and cook for 2 hours, stirring occasionally until rice is very soft and milk is absorbed.

Finely chop 1 large **onion.** Cook in a frying pan over medium heat in ¼ cup (⅛ lb.) melted **butter** or margarine until onion is golden but not browned; stir frequently (takes about 20 minutes).

Stir onions and butter into rice and let cool to room temperature. (Or you can make filling ahead and chill, covered; let it return to room temperature before using.) Makes about 3 cups filling.

Carrot or Cabbage Filling. Finely shred enough peeled **carrots** to make 6 cups (about 12 carrots) or enough **cabbage** to make 14 cups (about a 3-lb. head). In a large frying pan over medium heat, melt ½ cup (¼ lb.) **butter** or margarine. Add 1 large **onion,** finely chopped, 2 tablespoons **sugar,** and the carrots or cabbage. Cook uncovered, stirring frequently, for about 15 minutes for carrots or 40 minutes for cabbage or until vegetables are soft and begin to brown. Season to taste with **salt;** chill well before using. Makes about 3 cups filling.

Egg Butter. With a fork, finely mash 3 hard-cooked **eggs** (or force through a wire strainer). Blend with 10 tablespoons of soft **butter** or margarine. Serve at room temperature. (If made ahead, cover and chill.) Makes about 1 cup.

Pinch *rye pastry dough around cooked rice or vegetable fillings for* piirakka, *a Finnish hot sandwich.*

How to Grow Cress and Alfalfa Sprouts and Dill Sprigs

In Scandinavian kitchens, tiny window gardens supply a refreshing bit of greenery for garnishes throughout the year. Leafy cress and alfalfa sprouts or feathery sprigs of dill—all are used with the same frequency as we use parsley to make attractive and tasty garnishes for any open face sandwich or furnish a final touch for soups, salads, or such prepared dishes as herring, *gravlax*, meats, casseroles, and egg dishes. Cress sprouts have a nippy bite; alfalfa sprouts are crisp, mild, and a little grassy; and dill has its own uniquely mild and refreshing aroma and flavor.

Cress Sprouts or Alfalfa Sprouts

Cover the bottom of a small shallow dish (up to 2 inches deep) with a layer of cotton or white terry cloth or several thicknesses of cheesecloth. Saturate it with warm water and sprinkle evenly with a single layer of seed (see "Where to get the seed" below for a list of varieties). Place beside a window on the sill where the seeds are exposed to filtered light.

Within 24 to 36 hours, you will be able to see the seeds burst and the pale shoots emerge. From then on, the sprouts grow so fast you can almost see it happening. Keep the cotton or cheesecloth moist but not submerged, adding warm water as needed.

After 4 to 5 days, when bright green leaves have fully opened, brush the tops lightly to remove any clinging seed cases. To use, snip off or pluck sprouts; they may be harvested for about a 10 to 12-day period. Once cut, the plant is finished. For a constant supply, replant every two weeks. The yield from 1 tablespoon of seed is about 2 cups of cress sprouts or 4 cups of alfalfa sprouts.

Dill Sprigs

Fill a pot, flat, or other container having drainage holes with potting soil. Scatter dill seeds over the soil surface about ½ inch apart; cover with ⅛ inch of soil. Immerse the container in water almost up to the brim until all the soil is moist. Place on a drain pan in a warm place until the seeds germinate (8 to 12 days). Then move to a well lighted window or place under a fluorescent plant lamp until the weather is mild enough to set plants outdoors.

When the feathery leaves are about 4 inches tall, you can pinch off a few branchlets at a time from each plant (leave 1 or 2 big leaves on each plant at all times). When plants begin to look straggly, start a new crop from seeds.

Where to get the seed. Alfalfa seeds are available at health food or natural food stores. You may have to order the cress seeds (choose curled cress, upland cress, pepper grass, or broad-leafed cress—true water-cress sprouts have less flavor) through W. Atlee Burpee Co., Riverside, Calif. 92502. Dill seeds are available where garden seeds are sold.

Pick *tender, green sprigs of fresh dill to garnish sandwiches and many other foods.*

Soups & Salads

Light or hearty, festive or humble, quick or complex

Certainly you'll find much in these recipes for soups and salads that is familiar. They contain everyday ingredients, and the cooking techniques are those you know well. Even so, these dishes might well appear on tables tonight anywhere in Scandinavia. Where a recipe is a particular specialty of only one country, we mention it in the text.

In this chapter you'll find soups that are light and others that are filling; most in both categories are quick to prepare. The salads are mainly hearty mixtures, some of which can be used for a main course.

You can choose a soup and a salad to serve together as a meal. In some cases the soup might be the main dish; in others, the salad makes the entrée. Or you can serve a soup or salad with handsome Scandinavian-style open-faced sandwiches or main dishes from some other chapter.

There are also menu suggestions for combinations that Scandinavians find pleasing, but there's no need to wait for a party, a particular day, or date to serve anything here.

Soups

Winter is long and hard in Scandinavia, and a good hot soup helps ward off the cold. But winter isn't the only soup season.

The Finns celebrate the first summer vegetables by making them into soup. In Sweden, tradition calls for pea soup on Thursdays.

There's nothing very strange about the soups that follow. They recall the rich mixtures that once simmered on the back of the stove in Maine or Kansas or Oregon. You may notice a Russian influence in the beet or fish soups, but most of these recipes could have come from your grandmother's recipe book just as well as from Bergen or Goteborg.

Make a meal of the fish or meat and vegetable soups and good buttered bread, or serve drinkable soups in mugs with a plate of cold meats and cheese or a selection of hot sausages. And a bowl of soup served as a first course makes an otherwise plain meal fancy.

Dilled Green Pea Soup

Fresh, light, and quick to make, this is a soup you can serve in mugs for sipping.

Simmer together, uncovered, for about 10 minutes 2 packages (10 oz. *each*) frozen **peas,** 2 cans (about 14 oz. *each*) regular-strength **chicken broth,** ¼ teaspoon *each* **salt** and dried **dill weed** (or ¾ teaspoon chopped fresh dill). Whirl in a blender until smooth or press through a wire strainer. Reheat, stirring. Makes 6 first course servings.

Carrot Soup

This smooth golden soup has a springlike flavor, but you can find the ingredients anytime. It's a good first course—light but not too filling.

- 4 **pounds bony chicken pieces (backs, wings, necks)**
- 6 **or 8 sprigs parsley**
- 10 **or 12 medium-sized carrots, peeled**
- 2 **large onions, sliced**
  About 2 teaspoons salt
- 8 **cups water**
- 1 **cup whipping cream**
  About ¼ teaspoon ground nutmeg

Tie chicken and parsley in a bag formed from a single thickness of cheesecloth. Place in a deep kettle. Add carrots, onions, 1½ teaspoons of the salt, and the water. Cover, bring to a boil, and simmer slowly for 2 hours. Let cool slightly, then lift bag from broth and drain well. Discard bones and parsley.

Remove carrots and onions from broth with a slotted spoon and whirl in a blender with some of the broth until smooth (or force through a wire strainer). Return vegetable purée to broth in pan, stir in cream, ¼ teaspoon of the nutmeg, and additional salt if needed. (You can do this much a day ahead and chill soup, covered, overnight.) Heat to simmering. Ladle hot soup into bowls or mugs, and dust each serving lightly with nutmeg. Makes 12 to 13 cups or 10 to 12 first course servings.

Beet-Cabbage Soup

(*Punajuurikaalikeitto*)

This soup has a Finnish name but is common through all of Scandinavia. It's quick to make and light enough to round out a luncheon in combination with an Opera Sandwich (see page 9) or a sandwich of corned beef thickly piled on rye bread.

- 4 **cups regular-strength beef broth**
- 1 **small head (about 1¼ lbs.) cabbage, shredded**
- 1 **tablespoon lemon juice**
- 3 **large beets, peeled and shredded**
- ⅛ **teaspoon caraway seeds**
- ⅛ **teaspoon pepper**
  Sour cream and lemon slices

Bring broth to a boil and add cabbage, lemon juice, beets, caraway seeds, and pepper. Simmer, covered, 15 minutes. Serve with sour cream and lemon slices. Makes 4 to 6 first course servings.

Fish and Potato Selyanka

Finland became independent of Russia in 1917, but many Russian foods are still popular in Finnish kitchens. An example is *selyanka* (or *selianka, solianka, soljanka,* as you prefer)—the name given to a number of dishes that combine meat or fish with vegetables. The consistency of these dishes ranges from thick and stewlike to thin and soupy; the seasoning is often tangy. Offer Finnish Farmer Bread (see page 52) or other sturdy bread with this hearty fish and vegetable *selyanka*.

    2 pounds halibut steaks or Greenland
         turbot fillets
    6 cups regular-strength chicken broth
    1 pound new potatoes, peeled and cut
         in ½-inch cubes
    1 large onion, finely chopped
    1 teaspoon dried dill weed (or 1
         tablespoon chopped fresh dill)
    1 medium-sized white or red onion
         (mild flavor, if available),
         chopped
    6 tablespoons melted butter or
         margarine
       Salt and pepper
       Dried dill weed or chopped fresh dill

Melted butter, *chopped onions, added to taste, flavor fish and potato soup popular in wintertime in Finland.*

Place fish in a saucepan and add broth. Cover and bring to a boil over medium heat; then reduce heat and simmer 2 to 4 minutes or until fish breaks easily when prodded. Set aside for at least 20 minutes (or you can chill fish in broth to intensify the fish flavor); then lift out fish with a slotted spoon. Remove and discard any skin and bones; cut fish in bite-sized chunks.

Return saucepan with broth to high heat. Add potatoes, the large chopped onion, and the 1 teaspoon dried dill weed (or 1 tablespoon chopped fresh dill). Boil, covered, for about 10 minutes or until potatoes are tender enough to mash. Add fish and heat through.

Ladle soup into bowls; add to individual servings the chopped uncooked onion, melted butter, salt and pepper to taste, and an additional sprinkling of dill. Makes 5 to 6 main dish or 8 to 10 first course servings.

Salmon Selyanka

A lively balance of piquancy and sweetness in the soup provides an unusual and interesting background for salmon. It's a dish that goes together in just a few minutes. With a green salad, it makes a meal.

    2 tablespoons butter or margarine
    1 medium-sized onion, chopped
    2 medium-sized carrots, chopped
    1 teaspoon paprika
    3 cups regular-strength chicken broth
    1 can (1 lb.) stewed tomatoes
    2 tablespoons drained capers
    2 tablespoons sliced, pimiento-stuffed
         Spanish-style olives
    1 tablespoon vinegar
    1 teaspoon sugar
    1 large can (about 15 oz.) or 2 small
         cans (about 8 oz. *each*) pink
         salmon, or about 2 cups cold
         cooked salmon (skin and bones
         removed)
       Sour cream

Melt butter in a saucepan and add onion and carrot; cook, stirring, over medium heat until vegetables are soft. Stir in paprika; then add the chicken broth, tomatoes with juice, capers, olives, vinegar, and sugar.

Bring soup to a boil and simmer about 5 minutes, uncovered. Add salmon and any liquid, breaking fish into chunks; simmer 3 or 4 minutes longer.

Ladle into bowls and add sour cream to each portion. Makes 4 main dish servings or 6 to 8 first course servings.

Swedish Pea Soup

Traditionally, Thursday's main meal in Sweden is pea soup and pancakes. This soup takes several hours to cook but requires little attention.

Swedish yellow peas can be found at fancy supermarkets or in some delicatessens. Split peas can be used as an alternate, but they do not retain their shape.

Sort through 2 pounds of Swedish whole **dried yellow peas** (*östgöta*), discarding any extraneous materials. Rinse; then combine peas in a kettle (at least 10-qt.) with 14 cups **water.** Bring to a boil, cover, and set aside at least 1 hour (or overnight). (Or use 2 lbs. yellow or green split peas instead of the Swedish peas, omitting the boiling and soaking step.)

Add 3 large **onions** (finely chopped), 4 large **carrots** (finely chopped), 1 teaspoon **cumin seed;** bring to boiling. Cover and simmer 1 hour. Add a 5 to 6-pound shank end, bone-in section of fully cooked **ham** and simmer for about 2 more hours; yellow peas should mash easily (split peas will have fallen apart). Stir occasionally to prevent sticking. (If you make soup ahead, remove ham from soup and let meat and soup cool; then chill covered. Reheat together (takes about 45 minutes) at simmer, covered.)

To serve, transfer ham to a platter, scrape surface clean of soup, and cut in slices. Accompany with prepared **mustard,** prepared **horseradish,** and **buttered bread. Salt** soup to taste and serve in bowls along with ham. Makes 12 to 14 main dish servings; serve leftover ham cold, soup hot.

Finnish Summer Soup

(*Kesäkeitto*)

In Finland, all the vegetables in a garden are planted at the same time. When the carrots are 3 inches long—about time to be thinned out—the Finnish cook gathers some with other young vegetables to make this soup, so it's made there at just one time of year—early summer.

Here, it's possible to enjoy summer soup at any season, whether you have a vegetable garden or

---

Swedish Thursday Soup Supper

You needn't restrict the serving of this meal for 12 only to Thursdays, of course.

**A Whole-Tray-at-Once
of Sandwiches (see page 7)
Swedish Pea Soup (see this page)
Corn Rye or *Rågbröd* (see
page 52) or *Vörtbröd* (see page 53)
Butter   Mustard   Horseradish
Swedish Pancakes (see page 71)
Whipped Cream
Berry Jam
Burgundy Wine**

The hearty soup can be completed the day before; the oversized, thin pancakes can be made even earlier; and the bread, if you bake it, can come from the freezer. Open-faced sandwiches, the first course, go together just before serving. It's a thrifty party menu since your only major investment is a modest section of ham.

---

not. You can use frozen whole baby carrots, frozen petit green peas, and frozen green beans in place of the fresh garden vegetables. Choose the ingredients available to you, mixing fresh and frozen or using all of one or the other.

4 to 6 small (about 1½-inch diameter) new potatoes, peeled and halved
2 cups water
About 1 teaspoon salt
¼ teaspoon pepper
4 tiny onions (about ¾-inch diameter), or 4 green onions, cut in 3-inch lengths
16 very young (3-inch) fresh baby carrots, or 5 medium sized carrots, cut in 3-inch lengths, or 1 package (8 oz.) frozen whole baby carrots
2 cups green beans, cut in 1-inch lengths, or 1 package (9 oz.) frozen cut green beans
2 cups fresh shelled tiny new peas, or 1 package (10 oz.) frozen petit green peas
2 tablespoons melted butter or margarine
3 tablespoons all-purpose flour
2 cups half and half (light cream)

(*Continued on next page*)

Cook the potatoes in simmering water, uncovered, for about 5 minutes; add 1 teaspoon salt, pepper, onions, carrots, and green beans and simmer 8 minutes more, uncovered. Add the tiny green peas and cook another 2 minutes or until tender crisp.

Blend butter with flour; then gradually stir in cream. Stir into the simmering vegetables and cook, stirring, until boil resumes and liquid thickens slightly. Salt to taste. Makes 6 first course servings.

Salads

The positioning and definition of a salad has changed through the years in Scandinavia. Until recently, salads were usually composed of vegetables and were served with the meat or fish as a side dish, or they were hearty dishes of cold fish or meat with rich dressings, served as a first course or in a *smörgåsbord* or buffet. Nowadays these salads might all be separate courses—or if nourishing enough, a light entrée.

Leafy greens were once rare except in summer and costly at other times. But improved transportation has changed all that as dramatically in Scandinavia as in the United States. The light and healthful green salad is frequently served in homes, although restaurants don't always offer it.

So you can feel confident that the addition of a fresh, crisp salad to a Scandinavian-style menu won't make it any less authentic. Dressings may be anything from oil and vinegar to rich, thick, mayonnaise-based mixtures.

Asparagus and Shrimp Platter

In Sweden, whole boiled crayfish (see page 42) are used instead of the shrimp to make this dramatic-looking appetizer. You might make the switch if and when you can get this fresh water crustacean.

21 to 24 shrimp (30 or 40-to-the-lb. size)
Boiling salted water
14 to 16 very large, fat asparagus spears, all trimmed about 4 inches long
⅓ cup *each* salad oil and lemon juice
¼ teaspoon *each* dried dill weed (or ¾ teaspoon fresh chopped dill) and dry mustard
½ teaspoon salt
Lemon wedges
Parsley or dill sprigs

Devein shrimp by inserting a slender wooden or metal skewer into the back in several places and gently pulling up through the back to draw out the vein. Cook, uncovered, in boiling salted water to cover until shrimp turn pink (takes about 5 minutes); let cool, then drain and shell the shrimp.

Lay asparagus spears flat and parallel in a wide pan in just enough boiling salted water to cover. Cook, uncovered, until asparagus is tender when pierced with tip of a sharp knife (takes 3 or 4 minutes); drain.

In a wide, rimmed dish, arrange the asparagus spears on one side (keeping spears parallel) and the shrimp on the other. Mix together salad oil, lemon juice, dill weed, dry mustard, and salt; pour over shellfish and vegetables. Cover and chill.

To serve, arrange asparagus on a large, round platter, tips pointed to the center in a pinwheel. Loop 2 shrimp over every other spear, 1 shrimp over each of the remaining spears. Allow at least 2 spears for each serving. Garnish with lemon and parsley. Makes 7 to 8 first course servings.

Artichoke Hearts with Blue Cheese Dressing

Offer as a separate course or with a simple roast of meat or poultry.

Cook 1 package (8 oz.) frozen **artichoke hearts** as directed on the package; drain well. Mix artichokes with ¼ cup **salad oil**, 2 tablespoons **vinegar**, 1 teaspoon minced **parsley**, ¼ teaspoon **salt**, and a dash of **pepper**.

Cover and refrigerate, stirring several times during chilling. At serving time, drain artichokes, reserving marinade.

Crumble 2 tablespoons **blue cheese** into ½ cup **sour cream;** mix until blended. Thin, as desired, with some of the marinade and pour over artichokes. Makes 4 servings.

Herbed Celery Root Salad

Beneath the wrinkled brown skin of the celery root (also called celeriac) lies a smooth, white flesh known for its distinctive crisp texture and subtle celery flavor. As a salad, it fills the same bill as potatoes.

Peel 2 pounds (about 3 medium-sized) **celery root** and rinse. Cut into ½-inch cubes and drop at once into boiling **salted water** to cover, with a lid on, until tender (bite one to test); takes about 15 minutes. Drain well.

Combine 6 tablespoons **olive oil** or salad oil, 3 tablespoons **white wine vinegar,** 1 teaspoon **salt,** 2 teaspoons **sugar,** ½ teaspoon **pepper,** 1¼ teaspoons **dry mustard,** 1 clove **garlic** (minced or mashed), ⅓ cup *each* sliced **green onions** and chopped **parsley,** and ¾ teaspoon dried **dill weed** (or 2 tablespoons chopped fresh dill). Mix well; pour over celery root. Cover and chill at least 2 hours.

Serve on **lettuce leaves.** Garnish with sliced hard-cooked **egg** and sliced **ripe olives.** Makes 4 to 6 servings.

Marinated Cucumbers

Simple treatments of cucumbers add a freshness to all-season menus in the Nordic countries. Variations are many of a basically similar preparation.

Thinly slice 2 large **cucumbers** or enough to make 2 cups. Leave cucumber unpeeled, score sides before slicing with tines of a fork, or peel, as desired, for decorative effect.

Place slices in a bowl with 1 teaspoon **salt.** Cover and chill at least 30 minutes or as long as 24 hours.

Drain off accumulated liquid. Season in one of the ways given below; serve from a bowl or a bed of **lettuce** leaves. Garnish with **parsley,** dill sprigs, cress or alfalfa sprouts, or strips of canned pimiento. Makes 2 cups or 4 to 6 servings.

Cucumbers in Dill. Mix ¼ cup **tarragon-flavored vinegar,** 2 teaspoons **sugar,** ⅛ teaspoon freshly ground **pepper,** and ½ teaspoon **dried dill** (or 1½ teaspoons chopped fresh dill). Mix with drained **Marinated Cucumbers** (see opposite column) and serve.

Creamy Cucumbers with Onions. Slice 1 medium-sized **red onion** and separate into rings. Mix onions and drained **Marinated Cucumbers** (see opposite column) with ½ cup **sour cream** (may be half unflavored yogurt) and 1 tablespoon **lemon juice. Salt** to taste and serve.

Cucumbers in Sour Cream Dressing. Blend ½ cup **sour cream** with 1 tablespoon **lemon juice,** 1 tablespoon minced **onion,** 1 tablespoon minced **dill pickle,** ¼ teaspoon **sugar,** and ⅛ teaspoon **pepper.** Mix with drained Marinated Cucumbers (see opposite column). Add **salt** to taste. Top with 3 or 4 minced or sliced **radishes** and serve.

Green Beans with Peppers

The contrasting textures of cooked beans and raw pepper topped with a creamy blue cheese dressing make an interesting salad.

Snip ends from 1 pound **green beans** and cut lengthwise, cook in boiling **salted water** to cover, without a lid, just until tender; takes 8 to 10 minutes (or use 2 packages, 9 oz. *each,* frozen French-cut green beans cooked according to directions on the label). Drain well. Pour over beans ¼ cup **salad oil,** 2 tablespoons **vinegar,** 2 teaspoons minced **parsley,** ¼ teaspoon **salt,** and dash of **pepper;** mix well. Cover and refrigerate; stir several times while chilling.

At serving time, drain beans, reserving marinade. Seed 1 large **green pepper** and thinly slice lengthwise; add to beans. Blend 2 tablespoons **blue cheese,** crumbled, with ½ cup **sour cream** and thin, as desired, with reserved marinade. Serve dressing separately or pour over salad before serving. Makes 5 to 6 servings.

Six-Salad Supper

Six colorful salads, each contributing to the completeness of the menu, combine to make this refreshing dinner for six to eight. It's fun to serve the supper outdoors in the summer or by the fireplace in the winter. All the dishes are prepared ahead and chilled until time to serve.

**Green Beans with Peppers
(see page 23)
Artichoke Hearts with Blue Cheese
Dressing (see page 22)
Shrimp with Curry Mayonnaise (see
this page)
Marinated Cucumbers (choose the
kind you like, page 23)
Marinated Mushrooms (see this page)
Danish Potato Salad (see this page)
Creamy Liver Loaf (see page 38)
Kuminost Cheese Sliced Ham
Rye Bread Crisp Bread
Citrus Fromage Coffee**

Set up salad for buffet service, accompanying with rye bread and crisp bread, butter, a chunk of kuminost (a cumin-flavored cheese), sliced cooked ham (about ¾ to 1 lb.), and perhaps the creamy liver loaf or slices of liver sausage (about 1 lb.).

For dessert, serve a pretty molded fromage (see pages 74-75) or individual dishes of fromage (see page 74) with homemade or purchased fancy cookies and coffee.

Marinated Mushrooms

A versatile mixture, these mushrooms are good as a relish, appetizer, or with meats.

Wash, drain, and trim ¾ pound small whole **mushrooms.** Or use 2 cans (6 or 8 oz. size) whole mushrooms, drained.

Put mushrooms in a deep bowl, adding 6 tablespoons **salad oil,** 3 tablespoons **vinegar,** 3 tablespoons minced **parsley** or chopped fresh dill, ¼ teaspoon **salt,** and a dash of **pepper.** Cover and let stand at room temperature 5 hours or more before serving, mixing frequently. Makes 4 to 6 servings.

Danish Potato Salad

Hot cooked potatoes soak up an oil and vinegar dressing as they cool; mayonnaise and colorful garnish are added at serving time.

Split 1 clove **garlic** and let stand in 2 tablespoons **salad oil** about 10 minutes, then discard garlic. To the oil add ¼ cup **tarragon-flavored wine vinegar,** 1 teaspoon *each* salt and **sugar,** and ½ teaspoon dried **dill weed** (or 1½ teaspoons chopped fresh dill). Peel 1 pound hot, boiled **new potatoes** and cut in ½ inch cubes. Pour dressing over potatoes, mix, cover, and chill for several hours.

At serving time, mix into the salad 2 **green onions,** sliced; 3 large **radishes,** sliced; 2 hard-cooked **eggs,** chopped; and ⅓ cup **mayonnaise.** Garnish with slices or wedges of 1 more hard-cooked egg and chopped **parsley** or dill sprigs. Makes 4 to 6 servings.

Herring Salad

(*Sillsallad*)

This herring mixture can join other herring preparations in a *smörgåsbord,* or it can be served as a salad.

Drain liquid from 1 can (1 lb.) **pickled sliced beets,** reserving liquid. Also drain liquid from ¾ cup (or 1 jar, 6 to 8-oz. size) refrigerated marinated snack tidbits, fat, or wine-flavored **herring** fillet pieces. Cut in ¼-inch cubes the beets, herring, 1 medium-sized tart **apple** (peeled), about ½ pound **new potatoes,** boiled and peeled (hot or cold), and mix all together. Blend in ⅓ cup finely chopped **dill pickle,** 1 small **onion,** finely chopped, and reserved beet liquid. Pour into a serving bowl or pack into a 4-cup mold. Cover and chill at least overnight or for as long as 2 days.

Serve from bowl or unmold. (To unmold, drain off some of the juice; then invert salad onto a rimmed dish.) Surround with **parsley** or dill sprigs, or cress or alfalfa sprouts, and garnish with **lemon** slices. Makes about 4 cups or 4 to 6 servings.

Shrimp with Curry Mayonnaise

Pink shrimp, golden curry dressing, and red tomatoes make a pretty first course or a main dish.

Drop 1 to 1½ pounds **shrimp** or prawns (30 to 40 per lb.) in boiling **water** to cover, adding 1 tablespoon **shrimp seasoning** (or use ½ bay leaf, several sprigs parsley, 3 whole black peppers, and 1 teaspoon salt). When shrimp turn bright pink (takes about 5 minutes), remove from heat and let cool slightly. Drain, peel, and devein.

Mix shrimp with 2 tablespoons **salad oil,** 1 tablespoon **vinegar,** 1 tablespoon minced **parsley,** ¼ teaspoon **salt,** and a dash **pepper.** Cover and chill.

Combine ¾ cup **mayonnaise** with 1 tablespoon **lemon juice** and 1½ to 2 teaspoons **curry powder** (to taste); cover and chill.

At serving time arrange shrimp on crisp **greens** or serve in individual lettuce cups. Serve with curry mayonnaise. Garnish with **tomato** wedges. Makes 3 to 4 main dish or 6 to 8 first course servings.

Marinated Baby Beets and Onions

Put beets and onions to marinate as long as a day ahead.

Drain 2 cans (1 lb. *each*) small **whole beets,** reserving 1 cup of the liquid. In a deep bowl, combine beets and liquid with 2 thinly sliced, medium-sized **onions** (mild flavor, if available), ½ cup **red wine vinegar,** 1 teaspoon dried **dill weed** (or 1 tablespoon chopped fresh dill), 1½ tablespoons **sugar,** ½ teaspoon **salt,** and ¼ teaspoon **pepper.** Let chill several hours or overnight. Makes 6 servings.

Tomato and Onion Salad

A simple salad, this is a frequent summer choice in Scandinavia. Use Beefsteak tomatoes, if available.

Cut 2 large **tomatoes** in ½-inch-thick slices; slice 1 medium-sized, mild **red** (or white) **onion.** Place vegetables in alternate layers in a shallow bowl. Mix together ¼ cup **olive oil,** 2 teaspoons **oregano leaves,** and 1 teaspoon **salt.** Pour over vegetables. Makes 4 to 6 servings.

Dilled Red Cabbage

This salad is also good in sandwiches—try it with liverwurst, roast beef, or corned beef.

Combine 6 cups finely shredded **red cabbage** with ⅓ cup finely chopped **onion,** 1 cup **mayonnaise,** ⅓ cup **Italian-style salad dressing** (or oil and vinegar dressing), 2 teaspoons dried **dill weed** (or 3 tablespoons chopped fresh dill), and **salt** and **pepper** to taste. Cover and chill salad several hours before serving. Makes 6 to 8 servings.

Apple Coleslaw

Freshly grated apple adds a pleasing fruitiness to this sour cream coleslaw. If you like a slaw on the sweet side, include the pineapple.

> 1 **cup whipping cream**
> 1 **cup sour cream**
> ⅓ **cup white wine vinegar**
> 1½ **tablespoons sugar**
> ½ **teaspoon salt**
>   **Freshly ground pepper**
> 3 **red apples (Winesap or Delicious)**
> 8 **cups finely shredded cabbage**
> 1 **can (13½ oz.) pineapple tidbits, drained (optional)**
> 1½ **tablespoons lemon juice**

Mix together whipping cream, sour cream, vinegar, sugar, salt, and pepper to taste. Finely shred 2 of the apples and add to the cabbage. If a sweet coleslaw is desired, add the pineapple tidbits. Combine with the dressing.

Place in a serving bowl, cover, and chill until serving time (up to 12 hours). Just before serving, slice the remaining apple, core it, and dip in lemon juice. Arrange apple slices in a pinwheel in the center of the salad. Makes 12 servings.

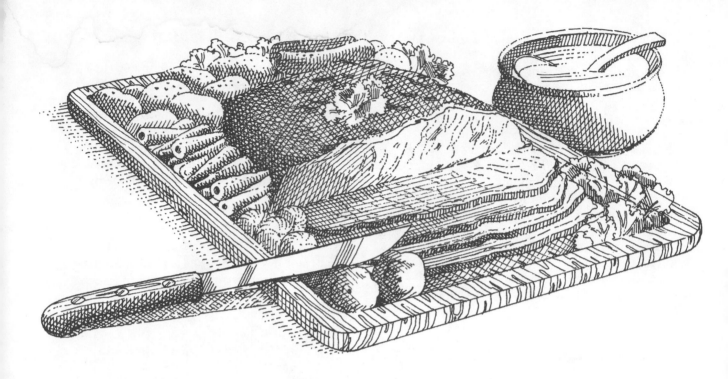

The Heart of the Meal

Meat, poultry, and fish—and foods to serve with them

The Nordic peoples eat more or less the same things we do—no kippered blubber or minced cat for them—but it's to be expected that, with their differences of climate and tradition, their cooking would offer us some pleasant surprises in the way of unexpected combinations of flavor or a switch in the way some familiar food is prepared.

A trait to admire in much Scandinavian cooking is thriftiness. If you're snowbound for months, a lavish hand in autumn may mean a hungry spring. So cooks have learned to create with whatever they have. A dish may not be costly, but that doesn't mean you can't serve it to company.

Scandinavian cooks often put the vegetables in to cook with the meat— a good way to save fuel and a method of cutting down on menu planning.

Since game and game birds are not available in our markets, we have adapted the recipes for these things to fit ingredients you can buy. Since we do have crayfish, though, and since there's no real substitute, we suggest you try catching some. Several crayfishing techniques are described on page 42.

Beef and Veal

The small Scandinavian countries, with their harsh climates and often rugged terrain, just don't lend themselves to raising beef cattle. Veal, of course, is a by-product of dairy herds—you have to do something with extra bull calves—but veal is expensive. So it's natural that these meats are served less often and in smaller portions than they are here.

One result of scarcity is that you do more with what you have, and Scandinavian cookery is full of good recipes for braised and chopped meats that would be a bit chewy in roasts or steaks. The meatball, for example, has achieved international renown in its many forms, and you'll find it here with other fine dishes, such as pot roast and stuffed cabbage.

Oxbringa

Oxbringa comes from the Swedish word for the beef brisket, the base of this colorful variant of a boiled dinner. It's a practical dish worth duplicating at home when you thin your vegetable garden or discover tiny new ones in the market. (Or you can use more mature vegetables and simply cut them into small pieces.)

Oxbringa makes an easy-to-manage entrée at a party for about a dozen guests. Cook the vegetables and make the creamy horseradish-seasoned gravy using the liquid in which the brisket simmered.

With the *oxbringa,* offer an oil and vinegar-dressed green salad and a light, simple dessert.

5 to 5½-pound piece fresh lean beef
      brisket
1 large onion, chopped
1 large carrot, chopped
6 cups water
1 bay leaf
6 whole black peppers
1½ teaspoons salt
1 tablespoon *each* celery seed and
      mustard seed
12 to 24 red skinned new potatoes,
      unpeeled (about 1 inch in
      diameter)
12 to 24 small white boiling onions
      (about 1 inch in diameter)
5 to 6 dozen Assorted Garden
      Vegetables (suggestions follow)
¾ cup whipping cream
3 tablespoons cornstarch
      Prepared horseradish

Trim excess fat from meat. Deeply brown meat without additional fat in a large (about 8 qt.) heavy kettle; since this is a large cut it will probably require shifting about in the pan in order to brown all surfaces. Lift out and set aside. Add the chopped onion and carrot to the drippings and cook, stirring, until lightly browned. Return meat to pan with the water, bay, pepper, salt, celery seed, and mustard seed. Cover and simmer gently for about 2½ hours or until meat pierces easily. (This much can be done ahead; cover and chill.)

Skim fat from broth or lift off solidified fat, if chilled; simmer meat in stock until hot through (about 45 minutes). Transfer hot meat to a serving platter; keep warm. Pour broth through a wire strainer; discard seasoning vegetables and spices. Heat broth to boiling, add potatoes and onions, and simmer, covered, for 5 to 10 minutes or until vegetables are tender when pierced. Lift out with a slotted spoon and arrange around meat; keep warm. Add your choice of the suggested garden vegetables and simmer, covered, for 5 minutes or until tender when pierced. Arrange around meat.

Blend cream with the cornstarch, add 2 tablespoons horseradish, and stir into broth; cook, stirring until thickened. Pass gravy in a separate bowl to spoon over meat and vegetables. Also pass additional horseradish. Makes about 12 servings.

Assorted Garden Vegetables. Choose at least 3 or 4 kinds from the following vegetables: small whole (about 3 inches long) **carrots**, **green beans**, **parsnips**, **crookneck squash**, or **zucchini**, or whole (1 to 1½-inch) **patty pan squash** or **turnips**. If you buy larger market vegetables, just cut them to pieces of similar size.

The Smörgåsbord

A *smörgåsbord* is a lavish way to dine and an easy meal to host. Quantities of hot and cold food are presented buffet-style and eaten with a certain ritual. The choice of dishes can vary, and the numbers of "plates" or steps can be enlarged—but the pattern is like the one followed in this meal. Herring, naturally, always comes first. Originally, the *smörgåsbord* was really considered just an appetizer course, with hot dishes and dessert following. Now, in homes, it frequently refers to the whole meal.

Here we have reproduced a *smörgåsbord* that a Swedish farming family set before us at Christmas time. You can make some dishes yourself or buy everything.

Our Swedish friends considered this a meal for four—but for a two or three-day period. You'll find it serves 10 to 12 generously on one leisurely occasion, with benefits that overlap into other meals. Invite guests to sample *smörgåsbord*-style as the menu suggests, visiting the table first to try the fish, then to taste the meats and cheese, next the main course, and finally the dessert.

Fish plate: Baked Smoked Herring (see page 14), Herring with Dill and Juniper (see page 14), *Inlagd Sill* (see page 12), Glazier's Herring, (see page 13), Herring Salad (see page 24), Boiled New Potatoes, Crisp Bread, Butter, Sour Cream

Meat and cheese plate: Liver Loaf (see page 38), Swedish Sausage, Sliced Head Cheese, Sliced Danish Salami, White Cheddar Cheese in Aquavit Towel, Rye Bread, Crisp Bread, Butter, Assorted Mustards

Main plate: Mustard-Glazed Ham (see page 35), Boiled New Potatoes, Salted Sliced Cucumbers. Sweet and Sour Red Cabbage, Pickled Whole Beets, Applesauce, Lingonberry Jam, Small Whole Dill Pickles, Rye Bread, Crisp Bread, Butter

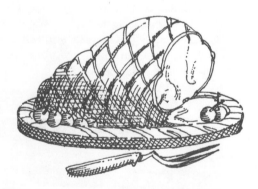

Dessert plate: Almond Tarts (see page 64), Berry Filling, Sweetened Whipped Cream

Beverages: Ale or Beer and Aquavit or Wine; Apple Juice or Milk; Coffee

How to assemble the Smörgåsbord

If you like, have fresh plates for each course.

For the fish plate: If you make all five herring dishes, you'll have enough for several meals. Or serve your favorite purchased prepared herring. Allow a minimum of 3 to 4 cups herring.

Accompany with hot, boiled new potatoes (see *For the main plate,* following), crisp bread (1 or 2 packages, 8-oz. size), and butter. Also have 1 or 2 cups sour cream to serve with cold herring.

For the meat and cheese plate: Prepare Liver Loaf or purchase about 1 to 1½ pounds liverwurst and slice. Serve heated about 1 to 1½ pounds Swedish sausage (or bockwurst) to cut in chunks. Also offer 12 to 24 slices head cheese and Danish salami or Lebanon bologna.

Purchase a 3 to 4-pound chunk white Cheddar or sharp Cheddar cheese and trim off rind. Bind circumference of cheese with a clean muslin towel and moisten cloth with about 4 tablespoons aquavit; chill in a plastic bag at least 4 hours before serving. Use extra cheese for snacking later.

Accompany with sliced rye bread (1 or 2 loaves, 1-lb. size), crisp bread, butter, and several mustards, such as Swedish, Dijon, or Düsseldorf.

For the main plate: Serve Mustard-glazed Ham or 3 to 4 pounds cold, sliced cooked ham.

Have boiled and hot about 5 pounds tiny new potatoes; keep on an electric warming tray.

Season 3 to 4 cups thinly sliced cucumbers with salt, sprinkle with chopped fresh dill or dried dill weed, and serve cold. Serve the following hot or cold: 1 can (1 lb.) sweet and sour red cabbage or 2 to 3 cups Red Cabbage in Port (see page 44), 1 can (1 lb.) pickled whole beets, and 1 can (1 lb.) applesauce.

Accompany with 1 or 2 cups *each* lingonberry jam and small whole dill pickles. Serve with some of the rye and crisp breads and butter.

For the dessert plate: Make the Almond Tarts or purchase 12 to 24 tart shells. Also get 2 cans (1 lb. 5 oz. *each*) cherry or blueberry pie filling and 1½ cups whipping cream; whip cream and sweeten. When ready to eat, spoon fruit filling into tarts and top with cream.

Swedish-style Pot Roast

Choose your favorite cut of beef for this flavorful pot roast.

> Beef chuck or rump roast, about 4 pounds
> 1 teaspoon *each* salt and ground allspice
> ½ teaspoon pepper
> 3 tablespoons butter or salad oil
> 2 medium-sized onions, sliced
> ½ cup regular-strength beef broth or water
> 2 teaspoons anchovy paste (optional)
> 2 whole bay leaves
> 2 tablespoons *each* vinegar and molasses
> 2 tablespoons cornstarch, blended smoothly with 2 tablespoons water
> 1 cup sour cream

Rub the meat on all sides with the salt, allspice, and pepper. Heat the butter or oil in a 4 to 5-quart kettle over medium heat. Put in the meat and brown well on all sides, adding onions about half-way through the browning. Stir in the stock with 1½ teaspoons of the anchovy paste, bay, vinegar, and molasses. Reduce heat, cover, and simmer until meat is tender when pierced (about 2 to 2½ hours). If you make this ahead, refrigerate meat with juices; reheat to continue.

Remove meat to a serving plate; blend cornstarch paste into sour cream and add to pan juices with remaining ½ teaspoon anchovy paste. Bring to boiling and stir until slightly thickened; serve with roast. Makes about 8 servings.

Ground Steak with Onions

Hakkebøf (*hock*-a-buff) is the Danish name for these beef patties topped with onions and rich cream sauce. They are special enough for a guest meal.

> 1½ pounds lean ground beef
> White pepper or finely ground black pepper
> All-purpose flour
> 1 tablespoon *each* butter or margarine and salad oil
> ½ cup whipping cream
> ½ teaspoon Worcestershire
> Slow-cooked Onions, hot (page 46 —1 recipe's worth)
> Chopped parsley or chopped fresh dill

Shape ground beef into 6 patties ½ to ¾ inch thick. Sprinkle lightly with salt and pepper; then coat with flour, shaking off excess. In a wide frying pan over medium-high heat, melt the 1 tablespoon butter and oil until sizzling; add meat patties and cook until well browned (4 to 5 minutes on each side for rare to medium). Transfer patties to a warm serving dish. Pour off most of the fat from the pan drippings and discard. Add cream and Worcestershire to pan. Cook, stirring to loosen browned particles, until cream is bubbly and somewhat thickened. Spoon Slow-cooked Onions equally over each ground beef patty; then pour sauce over all. Sprinkle with parsley or dill. Makes 6 servings.

Danish Hash with Fried Eggs

Biksemad (bick-sa-*mod*) is the name of this beef and potato hash. It makes a delightful entrée for a casual supper or brunch.

> About ½ cup (¼ lb.) butter or margarine
> 2 large onions, finely chopped
> 2 cups peeled cooked potatoes, cut in ½-inch cubes
> 3 cups cooked lean beef, cut in ½-inch cubes
> ¼ cup regular-strength beef broth or water
> 1 teaspoon Worcestershire
> ½ teaspoon salt
> ⅛ teaspoon pepper
> 4 to 6 eggs
> Butter lettuce and cherry tomatoes for garnish
> Coarse (kosher-style) salt (optional)

In a wide frying pan over medium heat, melt 3 tablespoons of the butter. Add onions and cook slowly, stirring occasionally, until they are limp and golden (about 15 minutes). When onions are cooked, transfer them to another container and keep warm.

Then, in the same frying pan over medium-high heat, melt 3 tablespoons more of the butter and cook potatoes, turning as needed to brown on all sides; add to onions and keep warm.

Add 1 tablespoon more butter to the pan and cook beef, stirring occasionally, until it is browned and heated through. Add beef to container with onions and potatoes; keep warm.

Again, using the same frying pan add broth, Worcestershire, salt, and pepper. Cook over high heat until reduced by about half; then pour over hash mixture. Mix lightly but thoroughly. Using the same pan, melt 1 to 2 tablespoons butter and fry eggs until done as desired. Spoon hash onto a warm platter and arrange eggs on top. Garnish with the lettuce and tomatoes. Serve with coarse salt, if you wish. Makes 4 to 6 servings.

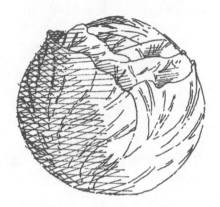

Beef-stuffed Cabbage Leaves

Meat-filled leaves may reflect the influence of the Mediterranean in Scandinavian cookery—but cabbage, rather than grape leaves, are what is available in the far north—and the flavors are very much of the Baltic.

Leftover rolls can be reheated in a covered casserole in a 325° oven for about 25 minutes. For crisp leaves, lightly brown leftover rolls over medium heat in enough melted butter to cover the bottom of a frying pan.

    1 large head (about 2 lbs.) cabbage
    4 quarts boiling, salted water
    1 pound lean ground beef
    1 medium-sized onion, chopped
 1½ cups cooked rice
    4 tablespoons melted butter or
          margarine
 ½ cup fine dry bread crumbs
 ¾ teaspoon salt
 ¼ teaspoon pepper
 ¼ teaspoon rubbed sage
       Tomato Sauce (recipe follows)

Cut out the core from the head of cabbage and discard outer leaves. Holding the cabbage under running cold water, carefully remove leaves one at a time, letting the water help you separate them without tearing. You will need about 12 to 14 leaves, depending on size (save the small inside leaves for salads). Immerse 4 cabbage leaves at a time in the boiling water, uncovered, just until bright green and limp (about 3 minutes). Remove leaves from water with tongs and allow to drain and cool.

For the filling, combine in a large bowl the meat, chopped onion, cooked rice, melted butter, bread crumbs, salt, pepper, and sage; mix until ingredients are thoroughly blended.

To fill the cabbage leaves, use 3 to 4 tablespoons of the meat mixture on the largest leaves; use 2 to 3 tablespoons for the smaller leaves. Place the meat near the base of each leaf; then, with the base of the leaf toward you, fold the leaf up over the meat and roll toward the tip. Hold the roll with the seam underneath and fold the outer edges of the leaf under, making a pillow-shaped roll.

Place the cabbage rolls in rows in a 9 by 13-inch greased baking dish; cover tightly. Bake in a 350° oven for 30 minutes (or 45 minutes if refrigerated). Serve with Tomato Sauce. Makes 4 to 6 servings.

Tomato Sauce. Melt 4 tablespoons **butter** or margarine in a small saucepan. Add ½ teaspoon **salt,** ½ teaspoon **chile powder,** and 2 tablespoons **all-purpose flour.** Stir to a smooth paste. Cook over direct heat until mixture bubbles, remove from heat, gradually stir in 2 cups **tomato juice,** and continue cooking over direct heat until it boils and thickens. Serve hot or reheat.

Basic Meatballs

Meatballs are to Scandinavians what hamburgers are to us—an everyday food, well liked, and served in infinite variety.

Meatballs should be light, tender, juicy—with or without sauce. They can be of any ground meat or combination of ground meats, and the extra ingredients that hold the juices may be bread crumbs, flour, potatoes, oatmeal, and similar products.

Here we give you a very simple starting point—good meatballs as they are—with alternate ways to cook, store, and reheat them. Then you can vary this recipe with the flavor changes suggested in recipes that follow. Serve with potatoes, rice, or noodles and a salad or vegetable.

Mix vigorously to blend (by hand or with an electric mixer) 2 pounds **ground meat** (may be all lean ground beef or up to half ground lean pork or veal) with 1½ teaspoons **salt,** ½ teaspoon **pepper,** 2 **eggs,** 1 cup **milk,** broth, or water, and *one* of the following: ½ cup **all-purpose flour,** ½ cup fine dry bread crumbs, 1 cup crumbled bread, 1 cup mashed potatoes (may be made from instant potatoes), or ½ cup regular or quick-cooking rolled oats.

Shape into meatballs with moistened hands (rinse hands frequently): this quantity makes about 160 meatballs, each ¾-inch diameter; 72 meatballs, each 1-inch diameter; or 36 meatballs, each 1½-inches diameter. Cook by one of the following methods. Makes 6 to 8 servings.

To pan fry meatballs, pour 2 to 3 tablespoons **salad oil** in a wide frying pan. Place over medium-high heat and add meatballs without crowding. Cook, shaking pan gently to turn meatballs (or turn with a spatula), until meat is no longer pink in the center; takes 10 minutes for ¾-inch meatballs and up to 15 minutes for 1½-inch meatballs. Remove meatballs from pan as they brown and set aside in a warm place until all are ready to serve.

To oven fry meatballs, place them slightly apart in rimmed baking pans (ungreased). Bake in a 450° oven until well browned: allow 10 minutes for ¾-inch in diameter or up to 15 minutes for 1½-inch diameter meatballs. Remove from pan with a wide spatula, transferring to a serving container.

To refrigerate meatballs, cover and chill. You can make them two or three days before you plan to serve; freeze for longer storage.

To freeze meatballs, let them cool completely. If you spread them out on shallow pans to freeze them, then place them frozen into airtight storage containers, you can simply pour out the number of meatballs you want to use at a time. Otherwise, freeze in airtight containers in quantities you plan to use.

To reheat meatballs, spread out in a single layer in a rimmed baking pan. Bake, uncovered, in a 375° oven; allow 10 minutes for ¾-inch diameter meatballs and as long as 15 minutes for 1½-inch diameter meatballs.

Norwegian Meatballs with Gjetost Sauce

Prepare Basic Meatballs (see opposite page) with all beef or equal beef and veal and 2 tablespoons **minced capers.** Shape into 1½-inch balls. Pan or oven fry.

If pan fried, remove as much fat from cooking pan as possible and blend in 2 tablespoons **butter** or margarine and 2 tablespoons **all-purpose flour.** Remove from heat and blend in ¾ cup **half and half** (light cream) and ½ cup **regular-strength chicken broth.** Bring to a boil, stirring, and cook until thickened. Mix in 1 cup shredded *gjetost cheese.* Turn heat low. Blend some of the hot sauce into ¾ cup **sour cream;** then return sour cream to sauce. Add 2 tablespoons chopped **parsley** or fresh dill.

If oven fried, discard fat and use some of the chicken broth to scrape free browned particles in pans. Make sauce with butter and flour and remaining ingredients in a saucepan, including the juices from baking pan.

Stir meatballs (they may be hot or cold) into sauce, simmering until heated through, and serve with cooked **rice** or cooked potatoes. Makes 6 to 8 servings.

Swedish Meatballs in Sherry Sauce

Prepare Basic Meatballs (see opposite page) using equal parts beef and pork; add 1 small **onion,** minced, an additional ⅛ teaspoon **pepper,** ⅛ teaspoon *each* **marjoram leaves** and **thyme leaves,** and ¼ teaspoon *each* **dry mustard** and **ground mace.** Shape meat in 1-inch diameter balls. Pan or oven fry.

If pan fried, discard all but about 2 tablespoons of the fat and blend in 2 tablespoons **all-purpose flour;** then add 1 can (10½ oz.) **condensed beef bouillon** and ½ cup **water.** Bring to a boil, stirring.

If oven fried, pour excess fat from baking pans, transferring about 2 tablespoons to a saucepan, adding flour. Then rinse baking pans with a little of the bouillon, scraping free browned particles, and blend this bouillon plus remaining bouillon and water into the flour. Bring to a boil, stirring.

Add meatballs (they may be hot or cold) and 2 tablespoons **dry Sherry** and bring to simmer; cover and simmer gently for about 10 minutes. Makes 6 to 8 servings.

Norwegian Meatballs with Red Wine Sauce

Prepare Basic Meatballs (see page 30) using equal parts beef and pork; add 1 small **onion,** minced, and ¼ teaspoon **ground allspice.** Shape into 1-inch balls. Pan or oven fry.

If pan fried, discard all but about 3 tablespoons of the fat and blend in 3 tablespoons **all-purpose flour.** Then stir in 1 can (10½ oz.) **condensed beef bouillon** and 1 cup **dry red wine.** Bring to a boil, stirring.

If oven fried, pour excess fat from baking pans; transfer 3 tablespoons of it to a saucepan with flour. Rinse baking pan with a little of the bouillon, scraping free browned particles. Blend this bouillon with the balance of the bouillon and wine in saucepan. Bring to a boil, stirring.

Add meatballs (they may be hot or cold) and bring to simmer; cover and simmer gently for about 10 minutes. Makes 6 to 8 servings.

Danish Frikadeller

Prepare Basic Meatballs (see page 30) using equal parts beef and pork. Add ¼ teaspoon **dry mustard** and ⅛ teaspoon **ground nutmeg.**

To make appetizers, shape mixture in ¾-inch balls and pan or oven fry. Impale hot or reheated meatballs individually on small wooden picks, each with a quarter slice of canned **pickled beet** on one side and a small piece of **sweet pickle** on the other. Place side by side on a tray and keep hot on an electric warming tray or over hot water in a chafing dish. Makes 12 to 16 appetizer servings.

To make a main dish, flatten 1½-inch meatballs to about ½-inch patties and pan or oven fry. Serve hot or reheated with **sour cream.** Makes 6 to 8 servings.

Veal Steak Novska

Sour cream and goat cheese are required for this rich amber sauce. They are blended into the pan drippings of sautéed meat. We suggest veal or chicken, but in Norway, venison, game birds, and reindeer often get the same treatment. It's company fare.

1½ pounds boneless veal cutlets or
     steak, cut ½ inch thick, or
  3 large (about 1 lb. *each*) chicken
     breasts, boned and skinned
  2 to 3 tablespoons butter or margarine
     Salt and pepper
  1 cup sour cream
  ½ cup shredded *gjetost* cheese

Trim any membrane from veal (or cut chicken breasts in half). Place meat pieces well apart on waxed paper, cover with another sheet of waxed paper, and then pound meat with a flat-surfaced mallet (or heavy bottle) until uniformly about ¼ to ⅓ inch thick (replace paper as needed).

Melt half the butter in a wide frying pan over high heat. Add meat, without crowding, and cook just until color turns light throughout, turning once; add remaining butter as required. Keep hot on a serving platter until all is cooked. Season with salt and pepper. When all the meat is cooked, drain any juices from platter back into pan and turn heat low. Stir sour cream and cheese with drippings just until cheese melts (do not boil); then pour over meat and serve. Makes 3 to 5 servings.

Pork, Lamb, and Variety Meats

Pork is particularly popular in Scandinavia, possibly more so in Denmark than in the other three countries. Sweet and piquant seasonings are quite typically served with this meat, whether it is roasted, pot-roasted, or stewed.

Ham, a special feature for many holiday meals, also turns up regularly on other less elaborate occasions, served hot or cold, for sandwiches, or to flavor such other dishes as soups.

Although lamb is prepared less often than beef, veal, or pork, it still contributes to the style of eating. Recipes here emphasize savory concoctions with sauces and seasonings that reflect home-style cooking.

Sweetbreads, liver, and other innards are prized and costly by our standards, and these recipes reflect the regard in which they are held. Especially good are the liver loaves (the French would call them *pâtés*) that make up part of the festive *smörgåsbord* and are handy for sandwiches, too.

Basic Pork Loin Roast

Serve the roast without adornment or choose one of the flavorful variations.

Select a 4 to 5-pound **pork loin roast** (center cut or loin or shoulder end). Sprinkle meat with **salt.** Place on a rack, fat side up in a close-fitting pan.

Roast, uncovered, in a 325° oven until a meat thermometer inserted in the thickest part of the loin registers 180° and there is no pink color next to the bone (cut a gash in a thick part of the roast to test); takes 2½ to 3 hours.

Transfer to a serving tray; skim fat from pan drippings and serve drippings along with the meat. Cut into chops. Makes 6 to 8 servings.

Pork Loin Chutney Roast with Potatoes, Danish style

Potatoes roast with the meat. You might also serve Glazed Carrots (see page 45) and Creamed Spinach (see page 44). A fromage or fruit soup from the final chapter makes an ideal ending for this meal.

Follow directions for **Basic Pork Loin Roast** (above) with these variations; before roasting, score the fat on meat in diamond shapes with a sharp knife. Measure out ⅓ cup **Major Grey's chutney** and snip through mixture with scissors to chop coarsely. Spoon chutney over meat, rubbing some of the liquid into ends and underside. Roast as directed; if surface begins to brown too deeply, drape pieces of foil over the dark sections.

Peel 4 large **baking potatoes** and cut in 1-inch cubes. Cover with boiling salted water and cook for 10 minutes, uncovered. Drain the cubes and spoon them around the roast 1 hour before meat is done. Stir potatoes to coat them with drippings. Baste potatoes occasionally with drippings during the remaining cooking period. Serve with additional Major Grey's chutney. Makes 6 to 8 servings.

Pork Loin Roast with Sour Cream Gravy

A pleasantly piquant touch in the sauce contrasts deliciously with the rich flavor of the pork.

Follow directions for **Basic Pork Loin Roast** (this page) with these variations: before salting, rub all over meat with ½ of a cut **lemon** and 1 cut clove **garlic.** Then sprinkle 1 teaspoon *each* **salt, marjoram leaves,** and ⅛ teaspoon **pepper** over meat. Roast as directed.

Transfer roast to a serving platter. Skim most of the fat from the pan drippings. Stir into drippings ⅓ cup **dry white wine** or regular-strength chicken broth and bring to a boil, stirring to free browned particles. Add ¾ cup **sour cream** and stir until sauce is warm. Do not boil. Spoon sauce over carved slices of the roast. Makes 6 to 8 servings.

Spiced Pork Roll

A Danish-style treatment of pork loin end roast turns it into remarkably lean, delicately seasoned meat roll. The simmered pork, weighted and chilled, can be sliced thinly and served for various occasions.

(Continued on next page)

At breakfast it makes a welcome change from ham or bacon. It also suits lunchtime menus, either at home or picnicking, and it's good for snacks anytime. If you like, serve the Green Mayonnaise as sauce for the meat, or spread the sauce on bread for sandwich makings.

The roll keeps well in the refrigerator for about a week, conveniently ready to serve.

    5-pound pork loin end roast, boned
    ½ teaspoon *each* ground allspice,
        ground pepper, and sugar
    1 teaspoon salt
    6 to 8 whole cloves
    4 cups water
    2 carrots, sliced
    1 large onion, sliced
    8 to 10 *each* whole black peppers and
        whole allspice
    Green Mayonnaise (directions
        follow)

Trim and discard as much fat as possible from meat. Mix ground allspice, pepper, sugar, and salt and rub into all sides of the meat.

Form meat into a compact loaf shape and tie securely at 1-inch intervals crosswise and lengthwise. Stud the meat with cloves. Set roll in a 4 or 5-quart kettle; add water, carrots, onion, whole peppers, and whole allspice. Bring to a boil, cover, and simmer 1½ hours; turn meat over once or twice while cooking.

Remove pan from heat, place a flat plate (or pie pan) directly on meat, and set a heavy weight such as a brick on the plate. Chill thoroughly. Remove meat from broth (save broth for soup or other uses) and cut away all the string. Serve or wrap in clear plastic wrap and keep in the refrigerator up to 7 days. Slice meat thinly. If desired, serve with Green Mayonnaise. Makes 8 servings.

Green Mayonnaise. In a blender jar, combine ¼ cup chopped, lightly packed **parsley,** ¼ cup chopped fresh, frozen, or freeze-dried **chives,** ¾ teaspoon chopped fresh **dill** or ¼ teaspoon dried dill weed, 4 teaspoons **lemon juice,** and ½ cup **mayonnaise.** Cover jar and whirl mixture until smoothly blended and pale green in color. Serve, or cover and chill until ready to use. Makes about ½ cup.

Pot-roasted Pork with Prunes

You can use apple juice instead of wine; if you do, omit the sugar.

    3 to 4-pound pork loin roast (center
        cut or loin or shoulder end), cut
        into chops and tied
    About 12 pitted dried prunes, cut in
        halves
    ½ teaspoon salt
    1 tablespoon sugar
    1 teaspoon ground ginger
    ½ teaspoon pepper
    2 beef bouillon cubes or 2 teaspoons
        beef stock base
    1 cup boiling water
    1 cup dry red wine
    2 tablespoons all-purpose flour
        blended with 2 tablespoons cold
        water

Untie the meat, distribute prunes evenly in the cuts; then retie roast.

Combine the salt, sugar, ginger, and pepper; rub all over meat and into cuts.

Put meat into a 4 to 5-quart kettle with fat side down. Cook over medium heat, turning until browned on all sides. Add the bouillon cubes, boiling water, and wine; reduce heat, cover, and simmer gently until meat is tender when pierced (about 2 hours). Remove meat to a serving dish and keep warm. Skim any fat from pan juices. Stir in the flour-and-water paste; bring to a boil, stirring until thickened. Serve gravy in a bowl. Cut the strings away from the meat. Makes about 4 to 6 servings.

Swedish Juniper Pork Stew

Gin, flamed, lends the woodsy flavor of juniper to this elegant pork stew.

Cut 2½ pounds **boneless pork shoulder** (or shoulder or loin end roast) into large chunks (about 1 by 2 inches) and sprinkle with ½ teaspoon **salt.** Brown meat well in its own fat in a wide frying pan over medium-high heat (takes about 20 minutes). Add 1 cup **water,** cover, and simmer about 45 minutes or until quite tender when pierced. (This step can be completed ahead. Cover and refrigerate the meat then bring to simmering over low heat to continue.)

Lift meat from juices and keep warm. Skim as much fat as possible from juices and discard; boil juices rapidly until they are reduced to about ⅓ cup. Add juices to meat.

Peel 2 medium-sized Newtown Pippin or **Golden Delicious apples** and cut in about ½-inch dice. Melt 2 tablespoons **butter** or margarine in the same frying pan and sauté apples on medium heat, stirring with a wide spatula, just until lightly browned and beginning to soften. Return pork and juices to pan.

In a small pan or long-handled cup, warm 6 tablespoons **gin,** pour over the meat, and immediately set aflame. (If the pan is beneath anything—particularly an exhaust fan—bring it out into an open area before flaming; return to heat as flames begin to subside.) Shake pan gently until fire dies. With a slotted spoon, transfer pork and apples to a serving dish and keep warm. Add ⅓ cup **whipping cream** to pan and boil on highest heat, stirring, until large shiny bubbles form (takes about 2 minutes). Pour sauce over meat and serve with **tart preserves** or jelly of rose hips, lingonberries, or cranberries. Makes about 5 servings.

Mustard-glazed Ham

Ham simmers, then chills, in a savory stock to enrich its flavor. The mustard glaze is a last minute dress-up touch.

Place a 6 to 8-pound bone-in section of fully cooked **ham** in a close-fitting kettle. Add 4 to 6 cups **water** (enough to come about halfway up ham), 6 **whole cloves,** 1 **whole bay leaf,** 2 large **onions,** cut in chunks, and 2 **carrots,** cut in chunks. Bring to a boil and simmer, covered, for 1½ hours or until a meat thermometer inserted into thickest section registers 140°. Let ham chill overnight in stock. Next day, lift off and discard fat; reserve stock for soup or other uses. If necessary, trim any rind and most of the fat from surface of ham. Place ham on rack in a roasting pan.

With a fork, beat together to blend 1 **egg,** 2 tablespoons **sharp mustard** (Dijon or Düsseldorf), and 1 tablespoon **sugar.** Spoon evenly over entire ham. Sprinkle with 1 to 2 tablespoons **fine dry bread crumbs.** Bake in a 350° oven for 30 minutes or until surface is lightly browned. Place the ham on serving platter; slice and serve. Makes 12 to 16 servings.

Lamb Chops Juniper

In Sweden, reindeer chops are prepared this way, too.

Trim most of the fat from 4 to 6 **lamb chops** (such as loin or shoulder chops, or leg steaks), cut 1¼ to 1½ inches thick. Place several pieces of the

fat in a wide frying pan over medium to medium-high heat, stirring until there is a film of fat in pan; discard chunks of fat. Sprinkle chops lightly with **salt;** then add to pan and brown on all sides. Allow about 12 to 18 minutes for slightly pink interior, longer for well done.

Pour ½ cup **gin** into frying pan and at once set aflame (if pan is beneath anything—particularly an exhaust fan—bring it out into an open area before flaming; then return to heat as flames begin to subside). Shake pan gently until fire dies. Transfer chops to a serving dish and keep warm. At once add 6 tablespoons **whipping cream** to frying pan and boil on highest heat, stirring, until large shiny bubbles form (takes about 1 minute). Pour over chops. Serve accompanied by a **tart jelly** or preserves, such as rose hip, lingonberry, or cranberry. Allow 1 or 2 chops for each serving.

Dilled Lamb Stew

If you'd like to serve just the stew meat with a separate dish of vegetables, omit celery and carrots.

Cut 2 pounds **boneless lamb** (shoulder or neck) in about 1½-inch cubes. Brown meat in its own fat in a large frying pan over medium heat. Skim out as much fat as possible and add ½ teaspoon *each* **salt** and dried **dill weed** (or 1½ teaspoons chopped fresh dill) over the meat and add 1½ cups **water.** Cover and simmer for 30 minutes. Then add 1 cup *each* sliced **celery** and sliced **carrots.** Continue cooking about 30 minutes or until the vegetables and lamb are tender. Blend 1½ teaspoons **cornstarch** with 1 cup **sour cream.** Stir into the stew; cook, stirring, until thickened. Serve, garnished with more dried dill weed or chopped fresh dill. Makes 6 servings.

Savory Lamb Roast with Mushrooms

Mushroom sauce makes a rich cream gravy for lamb shoulder roast.

> 3 -pound boned and tied lamb shoulder roast
> 1 teaspoon salt
> ¼ teaspoon *each* celery salt and pepper
> 2 tablespoons butter or margarine
> 2 tablespoons vinegar
> ½ pound mushrooms, sliced
> 1½ tablespoons lemon juice
> ⅓ cup half and half (light cream)
> 1½ tablespoons cornstarch

Rub meat with salt, celery salt, and pepper. In a close-fitting, oven-proof pan brown meat on all sides in 1 tablespoon of the butter. Add vinegar and cover. Bake in a 350° oven for 2 hours.

Melt remaining 1 tablespoon butter in a frying pan; add mushrooms and lemon juice. Cook over high heat, stirring, until mushrooms are limp and juices are evaporated.

Skim fat from the meat juices and pour juices into the sautéed mushrooms; bring to a boil. Blend cream smoothly with cornstarch. Stirring constantly, add to mushrooms and cook until thickened. Slice roast and serve with mushroom sauce. Makes about 8 servings.

Lamb and Mushroom Pirog

This lavish party entrée is complicated, but you can complete all or part of the steps well ahead of time. The dish is Finnish—but the influence clearly Russian.

> ½ cup warm water (about 110°)
> 1 package yeast, active dry or compressed
> ½ teaspoon salt
> 2 teaspoons sugar
> 3 eggs
> ½ cup (¼ lb.) soft butter or margarine
> 3½ cups all-purpose flour, unsifted
> Salad oil
> Lamb and Mushroom Filling, chilled (directions follow)
> 1 egg yolk beaten with 1 tablespoon water

Measure water into a large bowl and stir in the yeast. Let stand about 5 minutes; then stir in salt, sugar, and eggs. Cut butter in small pieces and add to liquid. Add the flour and mix with a heavy spoon until moistened. Shape into a compact ball with your hands and place on a floured board. Knead until smooth and elastic (about 5 minutes). Place dough in a greased bowl and turn over once to oil surface. Cover and let rise in a warm place until dough is about double in volume; takes about 1 hour.

Support *pirog* dough *with pastry cloth, flop over the lamb and mushroom filling. Seal and decorate with strips of reserved dough; then glaze and bake. Cut in rectangles and serve hot, or chill and reheat later.*

Knead dough on a lightly floured board to expel air bubbles. Pinch off a portion about ½-cup size and set aside. Shape the large lump of dough into a smooth ball. Lightly flour a pastry cloth (or heavy muslin towel) and roll ball of dough out on it to a rectangle 10 by 18 inches. Spoon cold Lamb and Mushroom Filling onto half of the dough at one end. Shape filling with hands into a compact rectangle, leaving about 1½-inch margin on the three outside edges. Using cloth to guide, lift the exposed section of dough over the filling. Neatly lap bottom edge up over the sides and pinch firmly around top rim.

Place a greased baking sheet without sides, top side down, on the *pirog*. Supporting with the pastry cloth and pan, invert *pirog* onto baking sheet.

Roll reserved dough into a rectangle about 3 or 4 inches by 12 inches and cut in ½-inch-wide strips, 12 inches long.

Arrange the dough strips decoratively over the top of the *pirog,* tucking the ends of dough beneath it with fingers or tip of a knife.

Let rise in a warm place for about 20 minutes. Brush exposed surfaces with egg-water mixture. Prick top of dough in 6 to 8 places with a fork. Bake in a 350° oven for 50 minutes or until dough is richly browned. Serve the *pirog* hot, cut in rectangles.

To bake ahead, cool hot *pirog* thoroughly on a wire rack. Wrap and chill as long as 24 hours. Place cold and unwrapped on an ungreased baking sheet, cover loosely with foil, and bake in a 350° oven for 50 minutes. Makes 6 to 8 servings.

Lamb and Mushroom Filling. Melt 3 tablespoons **butter** or margarine in a 4 to 5-quart kettle. Add 2 pounds thinly sliced **mushrooms,** mix with butter, cover, and cook over medium heat for about 5 minutes to draw out juices; stir mushrooms occasionally.

Remove cover, turn heat high, and cook, stirring frequently, for about 10 minutes or until all the liquid has boiled away. Mix in 2 tablespoons **all-purpose flour**, 2 teaspoons dried **dill weed** or 2 tablespoons chopped fresh dill, and ½ cup **sour cream**; cook, stirring, until bubbling and blended. Pour mushroom mixture into a large bowl and set aside.

Rinse frying pan and add to it 1½ pounds **ground lamb.** Cook over high heat, stirring and breaking up meat, until it is richly browned. Skim off and discard fat. Stir lamb into mushroom mixture, add ¾ teaspoon salt or to taste, cover, and chill thoroughly.

Sweetbreads with Mushroom Sauce

Serve over toasted English muffins or sourdough French bread for lunch or party brunch or serve from individual ramekins as a dinner first course.

>   2 **pounds sweetbreads**
>   **Water**
>   1 **tablespoon** *each* **salt and lemon juice**
>   **Swedish Mushroom Sauce (see page 45, one recipe's worth)**
>   **Toasted and buttered split English muffins (optional)**

Cover sweetbreads with boiling water; add salt and lemon juice. Simmer for 20 minutes; let cool in cooking liquid. Drain; peel off the surrounding membrane and remove tubes; separate sweetbreads into 1-inch pieces. Add to the mushroom sauce, cover, and simmer until hot.

Serve sweetbreads and sauce in individual dishes or on muffins. Makes 6 to 8 servings.

Swedish Tongue with Vegetables

Crusty, butter-browned slices of beef tongue, served with vegetables, make a whole meal.

>   **Cooked Beef Tongue and Broth (directions follow)**
>   **Salt**
>   1 **egg beaten with 2 teaspoons water**
>   **About ⅔ cup fine dry bread crumbs**
>   **About 7 tablespoons butter or margarine**
>   1 **large onion, finely chopped**
>   1½ **pounds asparagus, tough ends removed (or 2 packages - 9 oz.** *each* **asparagus spears)**
>   1 **package (8 oz.) frozen potato puffs, baked according to package directions**

Cut the cooked tongue in ⅜-inch-thick slices; salt lightly. Dip slices in egg; then turn in crumbs, shaking off excess. Heat a little of the butter in a wide frying pan over moderate heat and brown tongue on all sides; add more butter as needed. Keep browned tongue warm. At the same time, cook onion in 1 tablespoon of the butter with ¼ cup of tongue broth over moderate heat, stirring occasionally, until liquid evaporates and onion is slightly browned.

(Continued on next page)

In a wide frying pan (rinse the one used for the tongue), bring about an inch of the tongue broth to boiling; add asparagus and cook, uncovered, over high heat for 4 or 5 minutes or until stems pierce easily (or cook frozen asparagus as directed on package, using broth instead of water). Drain and salt lightly.

In a serving dish, arrange tongue slices, asparagus, and hot potatoes; garnish with cooked onion. Makes 6 servings.

Cooked Beef Tongue and Broth. Scrub well under running water a **beef tongue** weighing about 3 pounds. Place in a close-fitting, deep kettle and barely cover with **water.** Add 1 peeled, quartered **onion,** 2 peeled, sliced **carrots,** 1 teaspoon *each* **rosemary leaves** and **salt,** and 1 **whole bay leaf.** Cover and bring to boiling; reduce heat and simmer 3 to 3½ hours or until meat pierces easily with a fork. Cool in broth.

Peel skin from tongue and cut away fatty portions and any small bones at the base. Keep cold until ready to use. Pour liquid through a wire strainer; reserve broth and discard vegetables.

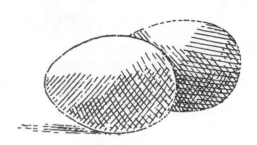

Liver Loaf

A country-style *pâté*, the meat mixture is slightly coarse and has a hearty flavor. Thickly sliced, it makes superb open-faced sandwiches; it also is a typical constituent of the *smörgåsbord.*

- ¾ **pound beef, baby beef, calf, or lamb liver (tough membrane cut away), cut in chunks**
- ⅓ **pound lean boneless pork, cut in chunks**
- 1 **small onion, cut in chunks**
- 1 **tablespoon anchovy paste**
- ⅓ **cup all-purpose flour, unsifted**
- 2 **eggs**
- ⅔ **cup whipping cream**
- ⅓ **cup melted butter or margarine**
- ½ **teaspoon pepper**
- 1 **teaspoon marjoram leaves, crumbled**
- 2 **tablespoons dry Sherry**
  About 1 pound sliced bacon

Force liver, pork, and onion through medium blade of a food chopper. Combine with anchovy paste, flour, eggs, cream, butter, pepper, marjoram, and Sherry; blend thoroughly.

Line a 6-cup-capacity loaf pan (about 4 by 8 inches) with bacon slices, extending slices over pan rim. Pour in the meat mixture. Fold bacon down over filling; then cover surface with additional bacon. Cover pan tightly. Set in a larger pan and place in a 300° oven. Pour 1 to 2 inches boiling water into the larger pan. Bake loaf for 2 hours (until it feels firm when pressed lightly in center).

Carefully remove from oven; discard water bath. Chill loaf thoroughly before serving. You can cover and refrigerate for 2 to 3 days; freeze, wrapped airtight, for longer storage. To unmold (thaw first, if frozen), dip pan to rim in hot water until sides begin to liquify. Invert onto a serving plate. Cut in thick slices. Makes about 2½ pounds or 10 slices, each about ¾ inch thick.

Creamy Liver Loaf

Richer and smoother in texture than the preceding liver loaf, this one is served in the same fashion.

Cook 3 tablespoons chopped **onion** in 1 tablespoon **butter** or margarine until soft. In a blender, purée the following mixture in several small batches: the cooked onion, 1½ pounds **calves liver** (cubed), ⅓ pound **bulk pork sausage,** 2 slices **white bread,** 1 cup **half and half** (light cream), 4 **eggs,** 1½ teaspoons **salt,** 1 teaspoon **Worcestershire,** and ¼ teaspoon *each* **ground cinnamon, ground allspice, ground nutmeg,** and **ground cloves.**

Spoon into buttered 5 by 9-inch loaf pan and cover top with foil. Place in a pan containing 1 inch hot **water.** Bake in a 350° oven for 1 hour; remove foil and continue baking 30 minutes longer. Cool; then chill. (You can refrigerate the loaf 2 or 3 days; wrap airtight and freeze for longer storage.) To serve, dip pan to rim in hot water until fat at edges just begins to liquify. Then turn out on a platter and garnish with sliced **olives,** hard-cooked eggs, and **watercress.** Makes 24 slices about ⅜ inch thick.

Poultry

In older times—and even in most places today—every farmyard had its collection of chickens, ducks, geese; and the hunter often supplied the table with game birds. Many of these creatures were cooked in their tender prime. But some managed to last to a tough old age, and the cook had a solution even then. Marketing has fairly well eliminated the likelihood of your finding a scrawny, stringy aged bird to tenderize. But the Swedish pot roasting technique applied even to young broiler-fryers will produce admirable results. You will also find in this brief sampling of poultry dishes a handsome way to present roast duck, a turkey to stuff, and complete instructions not only for roasting but also for carving the eccentrically assembled goose.

Roast Turkey with Sausage Stuffing

You can prepare the stuffing ahead. Refrigerate it, filling the bird just before roasting.

    1   pound bulk pork sausage
    ½   pound lean ground beef
    1   medium-sized onion, finely chopped
        Cooked Turkey Giblets (directions
          follow)
    ¼   cup chopped parsley
    ½   teaspoon *each* rubbed sage and
          thyme leaves
   1½   teaspoons salt
    ¼   teaspoon *each* pepper and ground
          allspice
    2   eggs, slightly beaten
    ½   cup milk
    4   cups cubed, firm white bread,
          toasted
   12   to 16-pound turkey
    2   or 3 tablespoons soft butter or
          margarine

Crumble sausage and beef into a frying pan; add onion and cook until all liquid is evaporated; then spoon out and discard fat. Finely chop the cooked turkey giblets; add to meat. Stir in parsley, sage, thyme, salt, pepper, and allspice. Beat eggs with milk; mix gently with meat mixture and bread. Cover and chill if made ahead.

Rinse turkey and pat dry. Spoon stuffing into neck and body cavities; skewer shut. Rub skin all over with butter. Set breast up on a rack in a roasting pan. Bake at 325° for about 2½ to 3 hours or until a thermometer inserted in the thickest portion of the breast registers 175° (185° in thigh). The leg joint should give easily when bone is jiggled. Let rest 30 minutes before carving. Carve turkey and spoon stuffing from cavities to serve. Makes 12 to 16 servings.

Cooked Turkey Giblets. Cover and simmer gizzard, heart, ½ onion, and 1 sprig parsley in a small saucepan with water just to cover for 30 minutes. Add liver and simmer 15 minutes more.

Parslied Chicken, Swedish Style

Browned in butter, then braised, these chickens develop a juicy flavor and a good sauce—simple but suitable for any occasion.

Rinse and pat dry 2 **broiler-fryer chickens** (2½ to 3 lbs. *each*). Rub the body cavity of each chicken with 1 tablespoon soft **butter** or margarine. Cut stems from 1 well washed bunch of **parsley.** Stuff half the parsley in each chicken. Skewer neck and body openings shut. Tie legs and wings securely to body.

Melt ¼ cup (⅛ lb.) butter or margarine in a 5 to 6-quart kettle. Brown chickens, one at a time, lightly on all sides over medium heat; takes 10 to 15 minutes each. Place breast up and add 2 cups **regular-strength chicken broth;** cover and simmer gently for 45 minutes or until flesh at thigh gives readily to pressure.

Carefully lift the chicken from the broth, draining juices from chicken back into pan. Place chicken on a serving platter. Keep warm.

Blend 1 tablespoon **cornstarch** with 1 tablespoon **water** and stir into juices, along with ½ cup **whipping cream.** Bring to a boil, stirring, until slightly thickened; season with **salt** and **pepper** to taste. Pour into a serving bowl.

Garnish chicken with more fresh parsley. Carve or cut into portions with poultry shears. Ladle sauce onto servings. Accompany the chicken with hot cooked rice, noodles, or small new potatoes. Makes 4 to 6 servings.

Danish-style Roast Duck

To serve roast duck in this unusual way, cut each side of the breast away from the bone and then heap seasoned mushrooms and juices into cavity.

4½ to 5-pound ready-to-cook duckling, thawed, if frozen
 Salt and pepper
6 to 9 small whole new potatoes
2 tablespoons butter or margarine
1 pound mushrooms, sliced
⅓ cup whipping cream
¼ teaspoon rosemary leaves
¼ cup finely chopped parsley
3 tablespoons dry Sherry
1 teaspoon *each* cornstarch and water

Remove giblets and neck from duck cavity and reserve for other uses. Rinse duck well; then pat it dry. Prick the skin all over with a fork and sprinkle inside cavity and on skin lightly with salt and pepper.

Place duck, breast up, on a rack in a roasting pan. Roast in a 350° oven for 1 hour. Remove duck from oven; discard all but about 2 tablespoons of the accumulated fat.

Set duck back in pan without the rack, add potatoes (2 or 3 depending on size, per person), turning them over in the drippings to coat them with fat. Continue roasting, basting occasionally with pan juices, for 1 more hour or until the duck is well browned, leg joint moves easily, and potatoes are easy to pierce.

Using two forks to support duck, tip and drain cavity juices into roasting pan. Arrange duck and potatoes on serving platter and keep warm. Scrape roasting pan, freeing browned particles; skim fat and discard.

Meanwhile, in a large frying pan melt butter. Add mushrooms and sauté over medium heat, stirring often, for 5 to 7 minutes. Stir in cream, rosemary, parsley, and salt and pepper to taste. Add roasting pan juices and cook, uncovered, over high heat until liquid is reduced by half. Mix in the Sherry. Blend cornstarch with water until smooth; then stir into mushrooms, and cook, stirring, until thickened.

To serve, run a small, sharp knife along either side of the breast bone and then under breast meat along rib cage; lay meat back. Spoon mushroom mixture into opening between bone and breast meat. Present; then carve or cut apart with poultry shears. Makes 2 to 3 servings.

Roast Goose with New Potatoes

Goose is a holiday dish, particularly in Denmark and southern Sweden, and because it's tricky to carve, instructions are included. Serve it with a garnish of Glazed Apple Slices and Prunes (page 45) and hot buttered broccoli.

Thaw completely, if frozen, a 9 to 10-pound **goose**. Rinse and wipe dry; remove any thick layers of fat from the cavities. Sprinkle inside with **salt** and **pepper**; stuff with 2 or 3 **onions**, quartered.

Skewer cavities shut. Tie drumsticks together.

Place the goose, breast side down, on a rack in a deep pan or use heavy foil to build up higher sides on a shallow roasting pan (it helps prevent oven splatter).

Roast, uncovered, in a 325° oven for 3½ to 4 hours or until thigh meat feels soft. Spoon or siphon off fat as it accumulates in the pan. For the last 1½ hours, turn bird and roast breast side up.

One hour before the goose is done, add 12 to 15 small, whole, unpeeled **new potatoes** to the pan drippings. Baste and turn occasionally until tender and lightly browned.

To serve, lift goose from roasting pan, remove skewers and string, and place breast side up on the serving platter. Use a slotted spoon to lift out the potatoes; pile them beside the bird (or keep warm while carving the goose). Spoon onions from cavity.

To carve goose, cut off the tips and first joints of the wings. Steady remaining wing section with fingers or fork and cut it off by forcing the knife tip at a 45° angle into the breast to the joint; sever by turning the knife while pulling on the wing.

A goose's hip joints are almost at the backbone. To carve the legs, turn the goose breast side down and cut through the back skin to expose joints; insert knife tip to loosen. Free meat from bone above the joints. Turn the goose breast side up and anchor a fork firmly in the thigh. Then cut between leg and body, pressing leg down horizontally—this should break loose the hip joint. Cut through to free the leg. Repeat for other leg. Separate thighs and drumsticks and then cut along the bones to divide each into two pieces.

Remove each side of breast by inserting the knife between meat and keel bone. Cut down to breast bone, along the wishbone, to wing joint. Cut meat free. Slice each breast crosswise into 2 or 3 servings. Serve goose and onions with warm potatoes. Makes 6 servings.

Fish

Scandinavia is a series of peninsulas and islands, their shorelines often deeply cut by narrow bays, or *fjords*. So it's no surprise that fish is such an important part of the Nordic diet.

Here, fish entrées get full attention: first some basic cooking techniques such as poaching, oven poaching, baking, and sautéeing. Following, at the end of this chapter, are a few fine sauces—subtle and rich, zesty and lean—that Scandinavians use with the cooked fish (as well as with other dishes).

Oven-poached Fish

This easy oven method permits you to assemble rather complex and delicate fish dishes ahead of time and with a minimum of fuss. To increase the number of servings, duplicate the procedure in additional baking containers.

Choose any one of the following relatively **lean, white-fleshed fish**: lingcod, Greenland turbot, halibut, giant sea bass, rockfish, or sole. You will need a total of 1½ to 2 pounds of skinless fish. Fillets should be no more than 1 inch thick, and steaks should be cut about 1 inch thick.

Arrange pieces, side by side, in a shallow, close-fitting baking dish or pan (size varies with shape of fish). Fold in half fillets that are less than ½ inch thick.

Pour ½ cup **regular-strength chicken broth** or dry white wine and 1 tablespoon **lemon juice** over fish; sprinkle lightly with **salt**. Cover and bake in a 400° oven for 10 to 22 minutes (shorter time for thin pieces, maximum time for thick pieces) or until fish flakes easily when prodded in thickest portion. Let cool slightly.

Holding fish in place with a wide spatula or pan lid, drain juices into a measuring cup; cover and chill fish.

You should have about 1 cup liquid, but this varies with the fish. Therefore either boil juices to reduce to 1 cup, or add broth or wine to make 1 cup. Use hot or cold as specified in the following directions for baked fish.

Baked Fish with Mushroom Sauce

A subtle sauce of cream, cheese, wine, and mushrooms balance in this delicate entrée. For a party menu, first offer cold artichokes, follow with the fish and a tart-tasting salad, and end with an elegant dessert.

Prepare **Oven-poached Fish** according to directions (see this page), using **dry white wine.**

In a frying pan, cook ½ pound thinly sliced **mushrooms** in 2 tablespoons **butter** or margarine, stirring, until mushrooms are limp and juices have evaporated; set mushrooms aside. Melt 2 more tablespoons butter in pan and blend in 3 tablespoons **all-purpose flour.** Remove from heat and gradually blend in the 1 cup **oven-poached fish liquid**, ½ cup **half and half** (light cream), and ⅛ teaspoon **ground nutmeg.** Bring to boiling, stirring, and cook 1 or 2 minutes or until thickened. Remove from heat, add mushrooms, and **salt** to taste. Let cool.

Spoon sauce evenly over cold poached fish, covering completely. Scatter ¾ cup shredded **Swiss** or **Jarlsberg cheese** over the fish. Cover and chill fish to bake later or bake at this point.

Bake fish, uncovered, in a 400° oven for 10 to 12 minutes or until sauce around edges is bubbling and cheese has melted. Dust very lightly with ground nutmeg and serve. Makes 3 to 5 servings.

Crayfish: How to Catch, Cook, and Eat

Various species of these mini-cousins of the lobster family are scattered all over the world. In many places—notably in Scandinavia—they are considered great delicacies.

Very likely you've heard both *crayfish* and *crawfish* as names for this creature. Both are correct. *Crawfish* is the usual form in much of the United States. Zoologists, however, use the term *crayfish,* and this also seems to be a colloquial choice in many parts of the Far West.

Crayfish are extremely adaptable. They inhabit creeks, lakes, rivers, canals—practically any unpolluted, year-around source of fresh water.

According to most crayfish connoisseurs, some of the tastiest are the five species belonging to the genus *Pacifastacus,* native to the western United States. They prefer streams and rivers.

The genus *Procambarus*, from the southern United States, is a more common crayfish. It favors still water—reservoirs, ponds, and lakes.

First check with state fish and game department as to regulations concerning crayfishing.

Since crayfish are most commonly found in slow-moving water between 1 and 10 feet deep, the most sporting way to catch them is to wade along a stream and when you see one, grab it. Or you can use simple purchased traps baited with liver or bacon.

The art of eating crayfish. There is no subtle way to eat crayfish. It is a two-handed operation. The tail, which breaks readily away from the body (or thorax), is the prize because it contains the major portion of meat. If the sand vein has not been removed, pluck it out. Those who take the time to crack the claws are rewarded with the sweetest, most succulent segments.

Juices that linger in the shells should be supped, and the body cavity cleared of its trove of sienna-colored "butter." In females you may find the delicious bright red egg clusters.

Very roughly we found that 10 to 12 crayfish (about 5-inch size) yielded about ¼ pound of tails or one serving.

Crayfish require special care; if you take them home, keep them cool and covered enroute with wet cloths or fresh, damp grass and then refrigerate up to 24 hours. Discard any that die before cooking (however, refrigeration makes them sluggish, so check reflexes carefully).

How to cook and serve crayfish, Swedish-style. Swedish cooks wouldn't think of masking the crayfish flavor with anything but the simplest seasonings, namely salt and dill.

Fill an 8-quart or larger kettle about half full of water. Add 2 teaspoons salt, a handful (20 to 30) dill sprigs or 2 tablespoons dried dill weed, and 2 cans (12 oz. *each*) beer or 2 cups dry white wine. Cover and bring to boiling. Simmer 15 minutes.

Meanwhile, rinse crayfish. To remove the sand vein before cooking (if desired), hold on behind the pinchers and twist the center section of the tail, snapping the shell; then pull out the sand vein and discard.

Return pot to vigorous boil. Uncover and drop in as many as 2 dozen crayfish, one at a time, big ones first. Push them down into the water to kill them quickly. When stock returns to a boil, cook 5 minutes or until crayfish turn bright red. Lift from liquid with a slotted spoon. Transfer to a platter. Continue to add crayfish to boiling pot, adding water as needed to maintain volume.

Crayfish are ready to eat as soon as they are cool enough to touch. Eat meat plain, dip morsels in melted butter, or accompany with mayonnaise.

Bright red crayfish *go from boiling pot to outdoor feast where they are the main attraction.*

Baked Fish with Horseradish Cream Sauce

Horseradish is used to add a surprisingly piquant touch to many unsophisticated-looking fish dishes, such as this one. Accompany with boiled new potatoes, broccoli, and a green salad.

Prepare **Oven-poached Fish** (see page 41) using **chicken broth**.

In a saucepan, melt 3 tablespoons **butter** or margarine and blend in 2 tablespoons **all-purpose flour**. Remove from heat and gradually add the reserved 1 cup **oven-poached fish liquid**, ⅓ cup **half and half** (light cream), and 1 tablespoon **prepared horseradish**. Bring to a boil, stirring, for 1 or 2 minutes or until thickened. Let cool.

Spoon sauce evenly over cold, poached fish, covering completely. Cover and chill fish to bake later or complete the baking at this point.

Bake fish, uncovered, in a 400° oven for 10 to 12 minutes or until sauce around edges is bubbling and fish is heated. Garnish with minced **parsley** or green onions (including some of the green tops). Makes 3 to 5 servings.

Fish Fillets with Mustard Sauce

The flavorful bits that remain after frying the golden fish are the start of this creamy sauce. Tiny, whole, boiled potatoes and Swiss chard complement this dish nicely.

      2 **pounds white, mild-flavored fish fillets, such as Greenland turbot or sole, cut in serving-sized pieces (thaw if frozen)**
         Salt and pepper
         About ¼ cup all-purpose flour
      4 **tablespoons butter or margarine**
      ¾ **cup dry Vermouth**
      ⅛ **teaspoon ground nutmeg**
      6 **teaspoons Dijon mustard**
      ¾ **cup whipping cream**
         Chopped parsley

Lightly sprinkle fish with salt and pepper; coat lightly with flour, shaking off excess. Melt 2 tablespoons of the butter in a wide frying pan over medium-high heat. Place fillets in a single layer in pan without crowding. Cook 3 to 4 minutes on a side, turning carefully until fish is lightly browned and is opaque throughout. Remove fish to a serving dish and keep warm. Add remaining butter and cook remaining fillets in same manner; keep fish warm while making sauce.

Pour Vermouth into emptied pan; stir to blend in browned particles. Turn heat high and stir in nutmeg, mustard, and cream. Boil rapidly, stirring until sauce thickens slightly and is reduced to about 1 cup. Pour sauce over fish and sprinkle with parsley. Makes 4 to 5 servings.

Danish Baked Salmon with Spinach

To go along with the salmon and spinach, you might serve small boiled new potatoes, sliced tomatoes, or a marinated cucumber salad (see page 23). Seasonal fruits are a proper final touch for this fresh-foods menu.

         About 3 pounds (4 or 5 bunches) spinach
   3½ **to 4-pound center-cut salmon piece, boned, cut in 2 fillets, and the skin removed**
      1 **tablespoon lemon juice**
         Salt
      1 **tablespoon butter or margarine**
         Lemon wedges
         Slow-cooked Onions (see page 46, and make ½ recipe), heated
         Whipped Horseradish Cream (see page 47)

Snip tender, fresh spinach leaves from stems into a quantity of cool water; discard stems and roots. Wash leaves in several changes of water, agitating to free any lodged bits of soil or sand. Drain spinach and set aside (if cleaned ahead, chill in a plastic bag).

Lay salmon fillets side by side, slightly apart, on a rimmed baking sheet; sprinkle with lemon juice and salt and dot with butter. Bake salmon, uncovered, in a 350° oven for 15 to 20 minutes or until fish has just turned an even, lighter pink color throughout and flakes readily when prodded gently with a fork in thickest portion.

After the salmon has cooked 10 minutes, put spinach in a kettle of at least 5-quart size. Cover and cook over moderate heat for a minute or two or until spinach starts to wilt and there is liquid in pan bottom; turn heat high and continue to cook until spinach is wilted, turning over frequently to cook evenly. Remove from heat, uncover, and keep warm. When salmon is also ready, lift spinach from pan with a slotted spoon, draining, and mound on a warm platter.

(Continued on next page)

Using two wide spatulas to support fish, lift salmon onto platter with spinach.

Garnish salmon with hot onions and the lemon wedges. Serve with Whipped Horseradish Cream. Makes 6 to 8 servings.

Fish Pudding

Norwegians call this type of dish a pudding or loaf and bake it in plain or fancy pans.

This particular pudding has a velvety smooth texture and subtle flavor. Serve it with Hollandaise Sauce or Whipped Horseradish Cream and asparagus for a luncheon or supper entrée.

> 1 **pound halibut, rockfish, or lingcod fillets (skin removed)**
> ½ **cup (¼ lb.) soft butter or margarine**
> 2 **eggs, separated**
> ½ **cup half and half (light cream)**
> ½ **teaspoon salt**
> ⅛ **teaspoon ground nutmeg**
> ½ **cup whipping cream**
> **Hollandaise Sauce (see page 47)**

Cut fish into 1-inch cubes, whirl in a covered blender until puréed (or force through the fine blade of a food chopper). Then add soft butter and blend until smooth. Blend in egg yolks, light cream, salt, and nutmeg. Beat whipping cream until stiff and fold fish mixture into it. Beat egg whites until stiff but not dry and fold in. Spoon into a buttered 1½-quart soufflé dish or fish-shaped mold. Set in a pan containing about 1 inch of hot water. Bake in a 350° oven for 25 to 30 minutes or until center of pudding appears firm when gently shaken. Let stand 10 minutes; then cover with a serving dish. Hold together and invert; lift off mold. Cut in slices and serve with Hollandaise Sauce. Makes 6 servings.

Poached Salmon with Sauce

You poach this fish conventionally, in water over direct heat.

Choose a saucepan that a 2 to 2½-pound chunk of **salmon** fits into compactly, but without crowding; wrap salmon loosely in cheesecloth and set aside. Place in pan 2 cups **water,** 1 cup **dry white wine,** 1 *each* sliced **carrot,** small **onion, celery** stalk, 1 teaspoon **salt,** 1 **whole bay leaf,** 6 **whole black peppers,** and ½ teaspoon **thyme leaves.** Bring to a boil, cover, and simmer 15 minutes. Lower fish into hot liquid. Return to boil; then simmer, covered, for 10 to 12 minutes or until fish flakes when prodded with a fork in the thickest section. Transfer salmon to a serving plate (use wide spatula to support, if needed) and remove cheesecloth.

To serve, garnish with **lemon slices** and dill or parsley sprigs. Remove skin and lift off chunks of fish. Accompany with Horseradish Butter (see page 47), plain Hollandaise, or a variation (see page 47). Makes 5 to 6 servings.

Side Dishes and Sauces

When it comes to vegetables, potatoes lead the list whether baked, boiled, mashed, pan fried, French fried, or hash-browned. And tiny, creamy-textured new potatoes would be our first choice as companions for almost any main dish in this book.

In addition to potatoes, vegetables from artichokes to zucchini are part of the Scandinavian repertoire.

Sauces for the vegetables and the main dishes also follow.

Red Cabbage in Port

An extremely popular vegetable dish to serve with any meat—particularly with fat, juicy sausages.

Finely shred a medium-sized head (about 1¾ lbs.) **red cabbage.** In a saucepan, combine cabbage, 1½ cups **Port wine,** and 1½ teaspoons **vinegar.** Add 1 **apple,** peeled and thinly sliced. Bring to a boil, cover, and simmer gently for 1½ hours, stirring occasionally; add a little more Port if cabbage becomes dry. Salt to taste and spoon into a serving dish. Makes 6 to 8 servings.

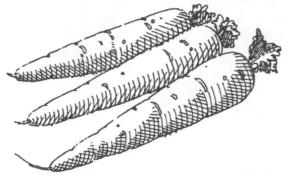

and thickly slice 3 large **apples** (Golden Delicious or Winesap). Melt ¼ cup **butter** or margarine in a wide frying pan, add apples, and cook over moderately high heat, turning gently with a wide spatula until fruit begins to soften and looks translucent (about 8 minutes). Sprinkle with 1 tablespoon **brown sugar** and ½ teaspoon **ground cinnamon** and cook, turning, until evenly glazed. Lift apple slices to serving platter; add prunes to pan and turn over in remaining syrup for 2 to 3 minutes to heat through. Arrange prunes among the apple slices, surrounding a roast if you like. Makes 4 to 6 servings.

These make a pretty accompaniment for meats on a platter or as a side dish.

Peel 16 small **carrots**. Cook in a covered frying pan in about ½ inch boiling **salted water** until just tender (about 10 minutes). Drain off cooking liquid. Add to the frying pan 1½ tablespoons **butter** or margarine and 4 teaspoons **sugar;** shake pan gently over high heat until carrots are lightly browned. Sprinkle with 2 or 3 tablespoons chopped **parsley.** Serves 6 to 8.

Jerusalem Artichokes with a Roast

Jerusalem artichokes, or sunchokes as they are known in some areas, have a nutty flavor and crisp texture. Cooked, they soften like a potato and develop a sweet, mellow flavor. Here they cook in the drippings of a roast—it might be beef, pork, veal, lamb, or poultry; the vegetable goes well with all of them.

Scrub or peel about 2 pounds **Jerusalem artichokes.** Cut each tuber crosswise in 1-inch-thick slices. About 1 hour before your **roast** is done (in a 325° oven), place slices cut-side down in the pan drippings. Baste and turn occasionally until very tender and lightly browned. Serves 4 to 6.

Glazed Apple Slices and Prunes

This hot fruit combination goes well with roast pork, duck, or goose.

Soak ½ pound pitted **dried prunes** in hot **water** to cover for 10 minutes. Drain. Peel, core,

Swedish Mushroom Sauce

Offer as a sauce for simply cooked meat, fish, or poultry, or as a side dish.

- ½ **pound mushrooms, sliced**
- 4 **tablespoons** *each* **butter or margarine and all-purpose flour**
- About ½ **teaspoon salt**
- ¼ **teaspoon white pepper**
- 1½ **cups half and half (light cream)**
- 1½ **tablespoons** *each* **lemon juice and dry Sherry**

Sauté mushrooms in butter until limp. Stir in flour, ½ teaspoon salt, and pepper. Add cream; cook, stirring constantly, until thick and smooth. Stir in lemon juice and Sherry; salt to taste. Makes about 2½ cups sauce or 3 to 4 servings.

Danish Crisp Onions

The Danes use their own special version of fried onions with a free hand to dress up servings of meat, fish, vegetables, or sandwiches. They buy these thin slivers of chewy-crisp, naturally sweet onions—quite unlike our own crusty fried onion rings—by the package, but you can make them easily at home. Store them in the refrigerator or freezer, ready to use as the occasion demands.

Peel and slice thinly 4 large **white-fleshed onions** (about 1½ lbs.). Separate slices into rings and place in a large bag with ½ cup unsifted **all-purpose flour.** Close bag and shake to coat rings.

In a deep 3-quart saucepan on high heat, bring 1½ inches **salad oil** to 300°. Add about ⅓ of the floured onions to the oil; cook about 10 minutes or until onions are golden brown. The temperature of the oil will come back up to 275° as the onions start to brown; regulate heat to maintain this temperature. Stir onions frequently. With a slotted spoon, lift browned onions from oil and drain on absorbent material; lift out particles that brown faster than others to prevent them from scorching.

Cook remaining onions in the hot oil, following this same procedure. Serve onions warm or cold. When completely cold, package airtight for later use. Store in the refrigerator up to 3 days or freeze up to 1 month.

Serve right from the refrigerator or freezer. Or to reheat, spread in a single layer in a shallow pan and place in a 350° oven for 2 or 3 minutes. Serve according to suggestions that follow. Makes about 8 cups or ½ pound; allow about ¼ cup for a serving.

With meat or fish. Accompany plain cooked **beef, pork, lamb, poultry,** and **fish** fillets or steaks with the cold or warm onions.

With vegetables. Sprinkle the cold or warm onions over servings of hot cooked and **buttered cabbage, carrots, cauliflower, corn, green beans, potatoes, Swiss chard,** or **zucchini.**

In sandwiches. Add the cold onions to cold **sandwiches** made of **chicken, liverwurst,** roasted **beef, lamb, pork,** or **turkey.** Or add onions to **frankfurters** and other hot **sausages** in buns or to cooked **beef patties** in buns.

Baked New Potatoes with Caviar and Condiments

In the winter, when a special fresh red roe is available in Scandinavia, this is a typical first course for a dinner—or for a light lunch, followed perhaps by soup, salad, or open-faced sandwiches.

Scrub small **new potatoes** (about 2½ inches in diameter) and allow 1 or 2 for each serving. Bake in a 400° oven for 40 minutes or until they give readily to pressure. Cut a gash in the top of each potato and press from sides to force open. Serve hot and pass the condiments; spoon some of each into each potato.

Condiments. For each 4 to 6 servings, present in individual containers 4 ounces lumpfish, whitefish, or salmon **caviar** (rinse, if desired, according to directions that follow), ½ cup hot melted **butter** or margarine combined with ¼ cup minced **parsley,** ½ to ¾ cup **sour cream,** and ½ to ¾ cup finely chopped **onion.**

To rinse caviar, pour into a fine wire strainer and hold under very cold running water; this reduces saltiness and removes excess food coloring. Drain and keep cold until time to serve.

Brown Sugar-glazed Potatoes

Cook 12 to 16 small **new potatoes** (about 2-inch diameter) in boiling salted water to cover about 20 minutes or until tender. Drain and peel. Heat ¾ cup firmly packed **brown sugar,** ¼ cup **butter** or margarine, and 3 tablespoons **milk** in large frying pan, stirring to blend. Add potatoes; shake pan over medium-high heat until potatoes are coated with some of the sauce. Makes 6 to 8 servings.

Slow-cooked Onions

Limp, golden, slowly cooked onions develop a wonderfully sweet flavor. They make a delicious topping for many vegetables—broccoli, green beans, zucchini, asparagus, peas; potatoes (mashed, boiled, fried); sliced meats; or open-faced sandwiches. Keep some in the refrigerator and use them freely.

Melt 3 tablespoons **butter** or margarine in a 10 to 12-inch frying pan; add 4 large sliced **onions,** separated into rings. Cook over moderate heat for about 30 minutes, stirring occasionally at first and more frequently as rings begin to develop a golden color. The onions should not show signs of browning for at least 15 minutes; if they do, reduce heat.

When onions are generally a light gold and a few bits are browned, remove from heat. Serve onions hot; or chill, covered, for 3 or 4 days, and reheat as needed. To reheat, put the amount you need in a small pan and heat, stirring. Makes about 1½ cups.

Hollandaise Sauce

This velvety sauce, plain or with additions, is perfect with an astonishing range of dishes. References to it are made through this book: serve on fish, meat, vegetables, sandwiches, and anything else that strikes your fancy. Use your blender or a beater to make the sauce; directions for both techniques follow.

Blender method. Melt ¾ cup (⅜ lb.) **butter** or margarine. Combine in a blender jar 3 **egg yolks,** 1½ tablespoons **lemon juice,** and 1 teaspoon **prepared mustard** (such as Dijon or hot). Cover and blend at high speed for a few seconds. Then remove lid and pour in the hot butter in a steady stream, slowly at first, more rapidly as mixture begins to thicken. Turn off blender as soon as all the butter is incorporated; prolonged blending can break the egg-butter emulsion and sauce will thin. Serve at once or at room temperature. If made ahead, sauce can be covered and chilled for several days. Bring to room temperature before serving, and if you want sauce slightly warm, set in warm-to-touch water and stir frequently (too much heat will also break the emulsion and make sauce liquid). Makes about 1¼ cups.

Whipped method. Follow preceding recipe, but use these techniques: combine **egg yolks, lemon juice,** and **mustard** in the small bowl of an electric mixer (or bowl in which you can use a wire whip with ease). Beat until well blended; then add melted **butter,** a few drops at a time at first, incorporating well with each addition. As mixture begins to thicken, you can increase the speed with which butter is added (if using a whip or hand rotary beater, you will either need someone else to pour in the butter, or need to stop briefly for each addition).

Hollandaise Sauce with Cucumber

A little cucumber and some herbs make basic Hollandaise into a perfect fish sauce.

Prepare **Hollandaise Sauce** by either the blender method or whipped method as given above. Stir into the warm sauce 1 tablespoon *each* finely chopped **parsley** and **chives** (fresh, frozen, or dried) and 1 cup chopped **cucumber** (if seeds are large, scrape out before chopping). Makes about 2¼ cups.

Dilled Hollandaise Sauce

Dill adds the refreshing fragrance and tang.

Make **Hollandaise Sauce** by either of the preceding methods (see this page), adding to the **egg yolk** mixture ¾ teaspoon chopped fresh **dill** or ¼ teaspoon dried dill weed. Reduce **butter** to ½ cup (¼ lb.).

Stir in ½ cup **sour cream** and chill. Makes about 1¼ cups.

Bearnaise Sauce

Tarragon and piquant bits of shallots lend zest.

Follow directions for **Hollandaise Sauce** (see this page) with these changes: before melting **butter,** combine ¼ cup minced **shallots** (or red onion) with ½ teaspoon **tarragon leaves** and 3 tablespoons **wine vinegar** (may be tarragon flavor). Boil rapidly, stirring, until liquid is evaporated. Then add butter and melt. Combine **egg yolks** with either **wine vinegar** or lemon juice and **mustard** and make sauce using either blender or whipped method. Makes about 1½ cups.

Horseradish Butter

Poached fish or boiled beef are often presented with this sauce.

Melt ½ cup (¼ lb.) sweet or regular **butter** and stir in ¼ cup **regular-strength chicken broth** or strained fish-poaching liquid (see page 41 or 44) and 2 tablespoons **prepared horseradish.** Serve hot to pour over foods. Makes about ¾ cup.

Whipped Horseradish Cream

Here's a fine sauce for baked or poached salmon—very good, too, with other fishes, such as lingcod and halibut.

Finely mash 2 hard-cooked **eggs.** Then mix with 1 teaspoon **Dijon mustard,** ½ teaspoon **prepared horseradish,** ¾ teaspoon fresh chopped **dill** or ¼ teaspoon dried dill weed, and **salt** to taste. Beat ½ cup **whipping cream** until just stiff enough to mound slightly. Fold in the seasoned egg mixture. Serve or chill, covered, for as long as 2 or 3 hours. (Blend before serving, if chilled.) Makes about 1 cup.

Breads... Plain & Sweet

Minor and major masterpieces, mostly from the oven

It is as a baker that the Scandinavian cook has earned the greatest and most deserved fame.

The wide range of breads is only sampled in this collection of recipes beginning with thin, unleavened breads, wafer-crisp flatbreads, the intriguing warm *rieska*, and soft and pliant *lefse* (that are very similar to the wheat tortillas of Mexico—except you start with potatoes). Rolls and loaves, made with yeast and mostly whole-grain flours, provide wholesome offerings to be enjoyed from the kitchen.

Sweet breads are a feast of forms for the eye as well as the palate. From countries rich in dairy foods, they are well fortified with butter and eggs—golden, fine textured swirls, braids, wreaths, trees, and pudgy buns; and Danish pastry, prepared step by step, or with a shortcut method.

You might make an occasion to share your own baking achievements by giving a coffee-table party in the Finnish fashion; enjoy some of the simple home-baked loaves with sausages, soup, or salad for weekday lunches; or make a beautifully shaped bread tree as the focal point of Christmas morning.

Flatbreads

Flatbread sounds odd, until you realize that any grocery store here usually has the Scandinavian rye-cracker bread long promoted for dieters. Additionally you'll often find the very, very thin rectangular wafer called "crisp bread" and the big, thicker rounds with the hole in the center (illustrated on the cover) called *knäcker bröd*.

Another crisp bread, actually called "flatbread," is one you can easily make. Each flatbread looks like an oversized cracker and is served in the same way—with soups or salads. Flatbread stores well at room temperature if kept airtight.

But breads that are flat aren't all crisp. The quick-to-make Finnish *rieska* is served while still hot and tender. And the Norwegian *lefse* can be served either crisp, or soft and pliable to wrap around the traditional foods suggested or any sandwich filling.

Swedish Buttermilk Flatbread

As you roll out each flatbread, turn over frequently to avoid sticking.

2¾ cups all-purpose flour, unsifted
¼ cup sugar
½ teaspoon *each* soda and salt
½ cup (¼ lb.) butter or margarine
1 cup buttermilk

In a bowl blend flour with sugar, soda, and salt. Cut in butter until mixture resembles fine crumbs. Stir in buttermilk, using a fork, until mixture holds together.

Shape into a ball with your hands and break off small pieces to make balls an inch in diameter; separate on a floured board. Roll out each ball on floured board to make a round 4 to 5 inches in diameter, turning dough over frequently to prevent sticking. Space rounds slightly apart on ungreased baking sheets. Bake in a 400° oven for about 5 minutes or until lightly browned; check frequently. Cool on wire racks. Store in airtight containers until ready to serve. Serve cold or warm.

To reheat, place in a 350° oven for 2 to 3 minutes. Makes about 6 dozen.

Norwegian Cornmeal Flatbread

In a bowl mix together 2 cups unsifted **all-purpose flour**, ½ cup **yellow cornmeal**, and ½ teaspoon **salt**. Rub in 4 tablespoons (⅛ lb.) **butter** or margarine until evenly mixed. Stir in ⅔ cup **water** and form dough into a ball.

Shape, roll, and bake as directed for Swedish Buttermilk Flatbread (see at left). Makes about 4 dozen.

Rieska

Rieska is an old-style bread in northern Finland and Lapland. You can make it quickly, and it's best freshly made, still hot, spread with butter. Serve it as you would any quick, hot bread, such as biscuits or muffins.

Rieska is made in various thicknesses—the farther north you go in Finland, the thinner you will find this bread.

You can vary the recipe by using barley flour, usually available in health food stores.

2 cups rye flour or barley flour
¾ teaspoon salt
2 teaspoons *each* sugar and baking powder
1 cup evaporated milk or half and half (light cream)
2 tablespoons melted butter or margarine
Butter

In a bowl combine the flour with the salt, sugar, and baking powder. Stir in the milk or cream and the melted butter until a smooth dough forms. Turn the dough out onto a well buttered baking sheet. Dust your hands lightly with flour, and pat the dough out to make a circle about 14 inches in diameter and ½ inch thick.

Prick all over with a fork. Bake in a 450° oven for 10 minutes or until lightly browned. Serve immediately cut in pie-shaped wedges and spread with plenty of butter. Makes 8 to 10 pieces.

Potato Lefse

Lefse is good either crisp or soft. Serve with butter, or with cheeses or preserves. One person can manage the shaping and cooking of *lefse,* but it goes best if a team shares the duties.

> About 2½ pounds baking potatoes
> Boiling water
> 2 tablespoons butter or margarine
> ¼ cup milk
> 1 teaspoon salt
> About 3 cups all-purpose flour,
>   unsifted
> Salad oil

Peel potatoes and cut into chunks. Cook in the boiling water to just cover until tender when pierced; drain. Mash potatoes or beat with an electric mixer until very smooth. Measure mashed potatoes; you need 4 cups. Add butter, milk, and salt and mix well. Let cool to room temperature.

Mix in enough of the flour (about 2 cups) to form a non-sticky dough; add flour gradually, the less the better.

On a floured board, shape dough into a smooth log and divide into 24 equal pieces; do not cover. Roll each piece of dough out on a floured pastry cloth or board to form a very thin round about 10 inches in diameter. Turn *lefse* over frequently to prevent sticking. If possible, cover rolling pin with a stockinet.

If cooking and work area are adjacent, you can easily roll out one lefse as you cook another. Or you can lay out the rolled *lefse,* side by side, on lightly floured waxed paper until all are shaped; then cook them.

Heat an electric griddle or frying pan to 375°, or use a griddle or large frying pan over medium heat. Lightly grease the griddle (as needed) with salad oil. To cook each *lefse,* shake off excess flour and place on griddle. *Lefse* should start to bubble immediately; cook, turning often with a spatula, until bubbles are lightly browned on both sides (about 2 minutes).

If you plan to serve the *lefse* right away, stack as they are cooked, wrap in foil, and place in a 200° oven to keep warm. Or cool completely on a wire rack, stack, and wrap well. *Lefse* can be stored, wrapped, in the refrigerator for a week (or freeze for longer storage). Makes 2 dozen.

For crisp lefse: Spread out in single layers on baking sheets. Bake in a 425° oven for about 3 minutes. Serve crisp *lefse* rounds (or irregularly broken pieces) in a basket to eat plain or with butter.

For soft lefse: Stack, wrap in foil, and place in a 350° oven 10 to 15 minutes. Keep warm on an electric warming tray or wrapped in a napkin. Serve soft *lefse* in one of the following ways: spread with butter and wrap around slivers of sharp Cheddar cheese or *gjetost* cheese; spread with sour cream, sprinkle with brown sugar, then fold to eat out of hand; spread with soft butter, sprinkle with cinnamon-sugar, then fold to eat out of hand; spread with sour cream, top with lingonberry preserves or other fruit preserves and roll up to eat with a fork.

Yeast Breads

Whole grain flavors dominate these recipes for rolls and loaves.

If the bread is at its very best warm, instructions are included so that you can make it ahead, then reheat. Keep in mind that the freezer is a very useful accessory for the cook who likes homemade bread on the table but doesn't want to bake every day. When you measure whole grain flours, spoon them lightly into the measuring cup and level with a spatula. Don't sift or pack these flours.

Graham Rusks

First you make the graham rolls; then you split them in half and slowly oven-dry them. The resulting rusks store well and are ready to serve.

Serve like toast, spread with butter or cheese. Or—a breakfast idea from Scandinavia—cover first with a layer of cheese (Camembert, Cheddar, jack, or cream cheese), then top with jam or jelly.

4 cups graham flour
3 tablespoons sugar
2 teaspoons salt
1 package active dry yeast
  About 2½ cups all-purpose flour, unsifted
3 tablespoons salad oil or melted shortening
2¼ cups warm water (110° to 125°)

In the large bowl of an electric mixer, combine graham flour, sugar, salt, yeast, and ½ cup all-purpose flour. Add oil and water. Beat at low speed, scraping the bowl sides, for ½ minute. Then beat at high speed for 3 minutes (or by hand 5 minutes). Work in 1½ cups more all-purpose flour with a heavy spoon. Turn out dough on a floured board (use all-purpose flour) and knead until smooth and elastic (about 5 minutes), adding more flour as needed. Place in a greased bowl; turn over to grease top. Cover and let rise in a warm place until doubled; takes about 1 hour.

Punch down dough; divide into 1¾-inch-diameter balls; pat each to make ½-inch-thick cakes. Set 1 inch apart on greased baking sheets. Cover lightly and let rise until doubled (about 30 minutes). Bake in a 425° oven for about 20 minutes or until lightly browned. Remove from oven; reset oven to 275°.

When the rusks cool, split them horizontally, using two forks. Return halves, cut side up, to pans. Bake in a 275° oven until crisp throughout about 2 hours. Store airtight for as long as a week and freeze for longer storage. Makes about 48 rusks.

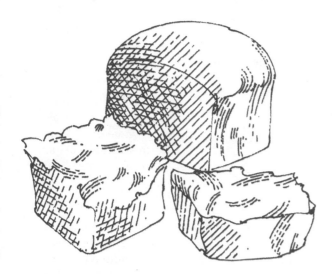

Swedish Raised Biscuits

(*Bullar*)

These Swedish breakfast biscuits, with their appealing, fragrant aromas of cardamom and warm yeast bread, stir almost any appetite.

You can make the simple dough and bake the biscuits (they might also be called rolls) and then store or freeze them to reheat for an early morning meal. Or you can offer them hot from the oven at midday.

Soft butter and comb honey go perfectly with them.

½ cup (¼ lb.) butter or shortening
2 cups milk, scalded
1 package yeast, active dry or compressed
½ cup warm water (about 110°)
  Whole cardamom
2 eggs
1½ teaspoons salt
½ cup sugar
7½ cups all-purpose flour, unsifted
4 tablespoons melted butter or margarine
  Milk

Stir butter into hot milk until melted. Set aside until just cool to touch (90° to 100°). Stir the yeast into the water and let stand about 5 minutes.

Break open cardamom pods and measure 1½ teaspoons seeds. Crush seeds in a mortar and pestle, a blender, or with the bottom of a flat-surfaced jar.

In a large bowl blend milk mixture, yeast mixture, cardamom, eggs, salt, and sugar. Add 1 cup of flour at a time; stir in as much flour as possible; then turn mixture onto a board with remaining flour. Knead all the flour in to make a smooth, soft dough; takes about 10 minutes. Add a little more flour to the board, if required.

(If you use a dough hook, add all the flour to mixer bowl and beat until dough pulls from sides of bowl; turn onto floured board and knead a few turns until a smooth ball is formed.)

Place dough in a greased bowl; turn over to grease top surface. Cover and let rise in a warm place until about doubled in size (about 1 hour). Place dough on a floured board and knead to expel air bubbles.

Pour melted butter equally into two 9-inch-square baking pans (or equivalent area). Divide dough in 40 pieces of equal size. Shape each biscuit, drawing edges under to make a smooth-topped ball. Turn balls in butter in baking pan, as you shape them, and arrange 20 pieces, smooth side up, in each pan. Cover without touching dough and let rise in a warm place until doubled in size (about 30 minutes). Gently brush tops of the biscuits with milk.

Bake in a 375° oven for about 25 minutes or until well browned; a thin wooden skewer inserted into center biscuits should come out clean. Serve at once or cool out of pan on wire racks.

To store, keep airtight for 1 or 2 days, or freeze; then reheat or split and toast.

To reheat, cover pan of biscuits with foil (or wrap this quantity in foil) and put in a 350° oven for about 30 minutes. If frozen, allow 40 minutes to heat.

Makes 40 biscuits.

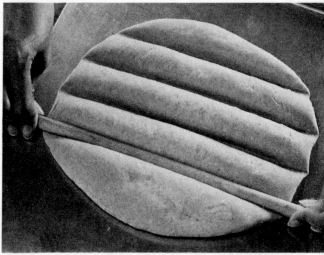

Form *break-apart lines in dough of farmer's style bread by pressing down with wooden spoon handle.*

Finnish Farmer Bread

Rye—one of the few grains that ripen in a short northern growing season—has been the staple flour in Finland throughout its history. Like most Finnish breads today, this simple yeast bread is made with part wheat flour and part rye flour, making the dough easier to handle.

If you are especially fond of heavy, firm breads, you may prefer the bread made with rye meal.

    1 package active dry yeast
    1½ teaspoons sugar
    1¼ cups warm water (about 110°)
    1½ teaspoons salt
    2 teaspoons salad oil
    2 tablespoons caraway seed (optional)
    1½ cups rye flour or rye meal
       About 2 cups all-purpose flour,
         unsifted
       About 2 tablespoons melted butter
         or margarine

Combine the yeast, sugar, and water in a large bowl; let stand for 5 minutes. Stir in the salt, oil, and caraway seed. Then add ½ cup *each* of the rye and all-purpose flours; beat with a heavy spoon (or mixer) until smooth.

Beat in remaining rye flour; then gradually mix in about 1 cup of the remaining all-purpose flour. When dough becomes too stiff to mix with a spoon or the mixer, turn it out onto a board lightly coated with all-purpose flour.

Knead until the dough feels very resilient and is no longer sticky, adding flour as needed; takes about 10 minutes. Place dough in a greased bowl; then turn over to grease the top. Cover and let rise in a warm place until doubled (about 45 minutes, or about 1 hour and 15 minutes if rye meal is used).

Knead dough on a lightly floured board to expel air bubbles; then cut in half and form each into a smooth ball. Place each ball on a greased baking sheet without sides and pat out to form an 8 or 9-inch diameter circle. Cover loosely with clear plastic film and allow to rise until almost doubled (about 40 minutes, or about 1 hour and 15 minutes if rye meal is used).

Using the handle of a long wooden spoon, form parallel rows in dough by pressing straight down to the pan in lines about 1 inch apart. Brush tops of loaves lightly with part of the melted butter. Bake in a 375° oven for about 35 minutes or until well browned.

Remove bread from oven, brush tops of loaves with melted butter; then place on wire racks to cool slightly. Serve warm or reheat, loosely wrapped in foil, in a 350° oven for 15 minutes. Makes 2 loaves.

Rågbröd

Rågbröd and the *Vörtbröd* that follows are two Swedish orange-flavored rye breads that typically accompany a Scandinavian *smörgåsbord*. *Rågbröd* is sweetened with honey; *Vörtbröd* is distinguished by the piquant flavor and light texture it gets from beer as an ingredient.

2 cups milk, scalded
2 tablespoons molasses
⅓ cup honey
1½ teaspoons salt
2 packages yeast, active dry or
    compressed
½ cup warm water (about 110°)
1 teaspoon *each* grated orange peel,
    crushed fennel seed, and crushed
    anise seed
3 cups rye flour
¼ cup (⅛ lb.) butter or margarine,
    melted and cooled to lukewarm
5 cups all-purpose flour, unsifted
1 egg white, slightly beaten

Scald milk and pour over molasses, honey, and salt in a large bowl. Let cool to lukewarm. Soften yeast in water; combine with milk and honey mixture. Beat in orange peel, fennel seed, anise seed, and rye flour. Blend in butter. Add 4½ cups of the all-purpose flour and stir to make a soft dough. Sprinkle the ½ cup flour on board and knead dough until smooth (about 5 minutes). Place in greased bowl; turn over to grease top. Cover; let rise in warm place until doubled (about 1½ hours).

Punch down, then knead on a lightly floured board just to expel air bubbles. Divide dough in half. To shape each loaf, roll each half to make a strand 28 inches long; fold strands in half, twisting one half over the other twice. Place twists well apart on lightly greased baking sheet. Cover; let rise until almost doubled (about 45 minutes). Brush with egg white. Bake in 350° oven for 45 minutes or until inserted wooden pick comes out clean. Cool on wire racks slightly before cutting. Serve warm or cold. Makes 2 loaves.

Vörtbröd

Beer contributes to the zesty flavor of these loaves.

2 packages yeast, active dry or
    compressed
½ cup warm water (about 110°)
2 tablespoons molasses
1½ teaspoons salt
1 teaspoon crushed fennel seed
1 tablespoon grated orange peel
2 cups beer
3 cups rye flour
2 tablespoons butter or margarine,
    melted and cooled to lukewarm
4¼ cups all-purpose flour, unsifted
1 egg, slightly beaten

In a large bowl soften yeast in water. Add molasses, salt, fennel seed, orange peel, beer, and rye flour; beat to make a smooth batter. Blend in butter. Add 3¾ cups of the all-purpose flour and stir to make a soft dough. Sprinkle last ½ cup flour on board and knead dough on board until smooth (about 5 minutes). Place dough in greased bowl; turn over to grease top. Cover; let rise in warm place until doubled (about 1½ hours).

Punch down, then knead on a lightly floured board just enough to expel air bubbles. Divide dough in half. Shape each half into a rounded loaf; place each on a lightly greased baking sheet. Cover; let rise until almost doubled (about 45 minutes).

Slash each loaf with razor blade to make a cross on top. Brush with egg. Bake in a 350° oven for 50 minutes or until well browned. Cool on wire racks slightly before cutting. Serve warm or cold. Makes 2 loaves.

Finnish Whole Grain Bread

(*Hiivaleipa*)

You can use all of one kind of whole grain flour in this bread, or try them in combinations.

1½ cups hot water
2 tablespoons butter or shortening
1 tablespoon sugar or honey
2 teaspoons salt
1 package yeast, active dry or
    compressed
½ cup warm water (about 110°)
3 cups whole wheat, rye, or graham
    flour
    About 2½ cups all-purpose flour,
    unsifted

Measure the 1½ cups hot water into a large mixing bowl. Stir in butter, sugar, and salt. Set aside to cool until lukewarm. Meanwhile, blend yeast with the ½ cup warm water; let stand 5 minutes. Blend yeast into the first mixture. Stir in the whole wheat, rye, or graham flour; beat for about 1 minute. Add 2 cups of all-purpose flour; blend to make a dough. Spread remaining ½ cup all-purpose flour onto a board; turn dough onto it, patting lightly all over with flour. Knead until surface is satiny and smooth; takes about 10 minutes. Add more flour if required.

Place dough in a greased bowl; turn over to grease top. Cover and let rise in a warm place until nearly double in bulk (about 1 hour).

(*Continued on next page*)

Punch down and knead on lightly floured board just to expel air bubbles; divide dough in half. Shape each half into a round loaf, place on a lightly greased baking sheet, and press down with hands until the dough is about 1 inch thick.

Cover and allow to rise about 45 minutes or until nearly doubled. Bake in a 400° oven for 25 to 30 minutes or until crust is light brown and a wooden pick, inserted in the center of the loaves, comes out clean. Makes 2 loaves.

Sweet Yeast Breads

A good variety of shapes for you to try—golden twirls called Lucia Buns, studded with raisins; fat, round, slightly sweet rolls to fill with slivers of almond paste and puffs of whipped cream; rich and easy to handle Finnish dough that becomes handsome braids, a tree, lively little dough people, and lavish wreaths; and then there are the Danish pastries with flavorful fillings.

Lucia Buns

Golden buns for the holiday season, to give or serve.

>   2 packages active dry yeast
>   ½ cup warm water (about 110°)
> 1½ cups warm milk (about 110°)
>   1 cup sugar
>   ¾ cup (⅜ lb.) soft butter or margarine,
>   cut in pieces
>   1 egg
>   ¾ teaspoon salt
>   ¼ teaspoon ground saffron (or use 1½
>   teaspoons ground cardamom and
>   1 teaspoon grated orange peel)
>   About 7½ cups all-purpose flour,
>   unsifted
>   About ½ cup dark raisins
>   2 egg yolks mixed with 1½
>   tablespoons water

In a mixing bowl combine the yeast and water; let stand 5 minutes to soften. Blend in the milk, sugar, butter, egg, salt, and saffron. Stir in enough of the flour (about 6½ cups) to form a very stiff dough. Turn dough out onto a lightly floured board and knead until smooth and elastic (about 10 minutes). Add balance of flour as needed to prevent dough from sticking. Place dough in a greased bowl, turn over to grease top, cover, and let rise in a warm place until double (about 1 hour).

Punch down dough, turn out onto a lightly floured board, and knead lightly to expel air bubbles. Pinch off balls of dough 1½-inch diameter and roll each into a smooth rope about 12 inches long. Place the rope on a lightly greased baking sheet.

For single S buns (sometimes called Christmas pigs or boars), coil ends of each rope in opposite directions; then stick a raisin in the center of each coil. For double S buns (sometimes called Christmas goat carts), form two S ropes as above, laying one across the other to form a cross. For triple S buns (sometimes called Christmas wagons), overlap three S ropes.

Cover buns lightly with plastic film and let rise in a warm place until almost double (about 25 minutes). Brush evenly with the yolk-water mixture.

Bake in a 350° oven until golden brown (about 20 minutes). Transfer to a wire rack. Serve warm; or cool completely, wrap and freeze. Thaw frozen buns unwrapped. To reheat, wrap in foil and place in a 350° oven for about 20 minutes. Makes about 5 dozen.

Swedish Semlor

Traditionally served for dessert on Shrove Tuesday, these sweet, cinnamon-flavored buns are also eaten on the remaining Tuesdays throughout Lent in Sweden. The buns, called semlor—and also Fat Tuesday buns or Fasching rolls—are filled with almond paste and whipped cream, and dusted with powdered sugar.

Serve to eat out of hand. More traditionally, put a bun in a bowl of warm milk and eat it with a spoon.

Lucia Festival—Celebration of Lights

Early on the morning of December 13, Lucia—Queen of Light—begins the Christmas season in many Swedish households.

Dressed in white, wearing a crown of evergreen leaves and twinkling lighted candles, she awakens her family with song and a tray of freshly baked buns and steaming hot coffee. Throughout the day other young Lucias with offerings appear in schools, factories, and at public gatherings.

The role of Lucia is often taken by the mother or oldest daughter in the family. In large towns and communities, a young girl is chosen to represent Lucia. Dressed in her regalia and attended by maids of honor, she passes through the streets singing during the day and into the evening.

The sources of this Swedish tradition are curiously mingled. The name of Lucia or Saint Lucia is presumed to come from the Italians; one of the songs commonly sung is "Santa Lucia." But there are also many pre-Christian aspects to the festivities.

Lucia Buns are typically flavored with saffron, adorned with raisins, and shaped in a variety of ways. The shapes and names of these buns can differ from one county in Sweden to another. Among the most popular is the simple S shape used in the recipe on the opposite page. The other two shapes suggested are variations.

Like Swedish families, you can make the Lucia Buns ahead and freeze them; then reheat them as desired to serve at any time during the holiday season. Serve plain or with butter.

Crowned *with evergreens and candles, Lucia maid offers hot Lucia Buns with coffee.*

⅔ cup milk
6 tablespoons butter or margarine
1 package yeast, active dry or compressed
¼ cup warm water (about 110°)
3¼ cups all-purpose flour, unsifted
¼ cup sugar
¼ teaspoon salt
¾ teaspoon ground cinnamon
1 egg
1 can or package (8 oz.) almond paste
1 to 1½ cups whipping cream, whipped and sweetened
Powdered sugar

Scald milk, stir in butter, and set aside to cool to lukewarm. Stir yeast into water and let stand about 5 minutes.

In a large bowl combine 3 cups of the flour, sugar, salt, and cinnamon. Add milk, yeast, and egg; beat well to make a soft dough. Knead dough on a board coated with remaining ¼ cup flour (add more if needed) until smooth and elastic (takes about 10 minutes). Place in a greased bowl; turn over to grease top. Cover and let rise until doubled in bulk (about 1½ hours).

Stir dough vigorously to expel air bubbles. Divide dough in 10 equal pieces and form each in a smooth, rounded ball. Place balls on a greased baking sheet about 2 inches apart; cover lightly and let rise until doubled (about 40 minutes). Bake in 400° oven for 15 minutes or until lightly browned; cool on wire racks. (Freeze, wrapped airtight, if made ahead.)

To serve, cut a thin slice off the top of each bun. Fill each equally with slices of almond paste and about ¼ cup of the whipped cream. Replace top; dust with powdered sugar. Serve at once or chill, covered, until time to serve. Makes 10 buns.

Finnish Cardamom Dough

Shape this dough into two braids for the coffee table (see page 59), one lavish tree for Christmas, four plump and golden dough boys to charm the young at heart, or two wreaths for any special occasion.

    1 package active dry yeast
    ¼ cup warm water (about 110°)
    ¾ cup warm milk (about 110°)
    ½ cup sugar
    ½ teaspoon salt
    2 eggs
    1 teaspoon ground cardamom
      About 4½ cups all-purpose flour,
         unsifted
    ½ cup (¼ lb.) butter or margarine,
         melted and cooled

In a mixing bowl combine yeast and water and let stand 5 minutes to soften. Blend in milk, sugar, salt, eggs, cardamom, and 2 cups of the flour. Beat until smooth. Then add butter and blend well. Stir in 2¼ more cups flour, beating to make a dough.

Coat a board with remaining flour and scoop dough out onto it; then pat flour over surface of dough. Knead until dough is smooth and satiny feeling (takes 5 to 10 minutes).

Place dough in a greased bowl; turn over to grease top. Cover and set in a warm place until about doubled in volume (takes 1½ to 2 hours).

Knead dough on lightly floured board just to expel air bubbles. Then shape and bake according to one of the following techniques:

Coffee Table Braids (*pulla*** or ***pitko***).** Divide Finnish Cardamom Dough (see above) into 6 equal portions. Roll each portion between your hands to make 14-inch-long strands. Place 3 strands side by side in the center of a greased baking sheet; braid from center to each end, pinching ends to seal and tucking slightly under loaf. Repeat to make the second loaf.

Cover lightly and set in a warm place until puffy looking (about 30 minutes). Gently brush all over with beaten **egg.** Sprinkle each loaf with 1 tablespoon coarsely chopped **almonds** and 1 tablespoon coarsely crushed **sugar cubes.** Bake in a 350° oven until richly browned; takes about 25 minutes. Cool on wire racks. Slice to serve. Makes 2 loaves.

Christmas Tree Bread. Divide Finnish Cardamom Dough (see above) into 16 equal portions. Roll each portion between your hands to make 12-inch-long strands.

From 1 strand cut two 5-inch lengths; set scraps aside. Butt the 5-inch pieces together at the center of one end of a large greased baking sheet, forming an upside down V that is to be the top branches of the tree. Curl the end of each "branch" upwards. Cut a total of 9 more pairs of branches, cutting each set ½ inch longer than the preceding one and fit in beneath the top branch, forming a rather solid center for the tree. Curl all branch ends, tapering out from the tip; reserve scraps from each rope.

Cut an 8-inch strand and fit into the base of the V, filling it in; do not curl ends.

Join all the remaining scraps of dough and form into a smooth ball.

Divide ball into 3 equal pieces and shape each into a 20-inch-long strand. Braid and lay down the center of the tree to conceal the joining of the branches and to form the trunk.

To decorate, press halves of **glacéed cherries** into the curl at the end of each branch.

Cover lightly and let stand in warm place until puffy looking (about 30 minutes). Brush all over with beaten **egg.**

Bake in a 350° oven for 40 minutes or until richly browned. Let cool on pan at least 10 minutes before transferring to serving tray. Or cool completely on pan; then wrap and freeze. Serve warm or cold. To reheat, place uncovered in a 350° oven for about 30 minutes. Pull apart to serve. Makes 8 to 10 servings.

Finnish Doughboys (*pullapojat***).** To make each doughboy, measure 2 portions, each ¼-cup size, of Finnish Cardamom Dough (see opposite column). Shape each in an 8-inch-long strand.

Place strands about 1 inch apart and parallel on a greased baking sheet; these strands become arms and legs. Flatten about a 1-inch section in the center of each strand with your fingers. Shape a piece of dough into a smooth 1-inch ball and place it against the center of one of the strands to make the head. Then make another ball of ¼ cup of the dough, shape like an egg, flatten slightly, and fit it against the head and across the arms and legs for a body. Bend arms and legs to show activity and add little pieces of dough to make hands and feet. To make a hat, use about 1 tablespoon of dough flattened into a small round cap or other hat style. Press cap lightly to head.

To make each doughgirl, measure a ¼-cup portion of dough and shape into an 8-inch-long strand and place on a greased baking sheet; flatten a 1-inch section in the center. Shape a smooth 1-inch ball of dough for head and place it against the center of the arms.

Make a 2 tablespoon-size ball of dough and place on the arms, against the head, to make the blouse. Then make another ¼-cup size smooth ball of dough for the skirt and place against the blouse.

Make each leg with a ¾-inch-thick strand of dough cut 3 inches long. Place side by side and tuck under skirt. Flatten blouse and skirt slightly with your fingers. Use little pieces of dough to make hands and feet.

For hair, make two strands of dough ¼ inch thick and 8 inches long; twist together and curve around the head.

Press dark **raisins** or currants well down into dough to make facial features and buttons for both doughboys and doughgirls. Cover lightly and let stand in a warm place until puffy looking (about 30 minutes). Brush all over with beaten **egg.** Bake in a 350° oven for about 30 minutes or until well browned. Serve warm or cooled; cool on wire racks. To store, wrap airtight and freeze. Makes 4 doughpeople.

Finnish Cardamom Wreath. Add 2 teaspoons grated **orange peel** to the Finnish Cardamom Dough (see opposite page) while mixing. After the dough has risen and has been kneaded to expel air bubbles, shape into 2 wreaths.

Divide dough in 6 equal portions. Roll each portion between your hands to make strands of equal length from 18 to 24 inches long. On a greased baking sheet, place 3 of the strands side by side along one edge. Braid from the center out to each end, then pinch ends together to form a wreath. Repeat to make the second wreath. Cover lightly and let stand in a warm place until nearly doubled (about 1 hour).

Brush braids all over with beaten **egg,** and if you like, sprinkle with 1 or 2 tablespoons chopped **almonds.** Bake in a 350° oven for about 30 minutes or until well browned.

Serve warm or cool on wire rack. (If you like, you can ice each slightly warm or cooled loaf—do not reheat after icing—by drizzling with this mixture: beat until smooth 1 cup unsifted **powdered sugar,** 2 tablespoons **milk,** and ½ teaspoon **lemon extract.**) To store, wrap airtight and freeze. To reheat, place thawed loaf, unwrapped, in a 350° oven for 15 minutes. Slice to serve. Makes 2 loaves.

Danish Pastry

(*Wienerbrød*)

Eating Danish pastry, many-layered, flaky, and buttery, is an international treat, but it's known in Denmark as *Wienerbrød* (Vienna bread).

The pastry is not difficult to make if you follow the directions precisely; the most important technique is to keep the dough cool so the butter retains a waxy texture during the many folding and rolling steps that make the lovely layers.

Make the fillings before you start the dough.

You have several options as to when to finish shaping or baking the pastries—all aimed at making an impressive presentation that suits your schedule and storage facilities.

> 2 packages yeast, active dry or compressed
> ¼ cup warm water (about 110°)
> 1 cup milk
> 1 egg
> 3 tablespoons sugar
> ½ teaspoon ground cardamom (optional)
> ½ teaspoon salt
> About 4 cups all-purpose flour, unsifted
> 2 cups (1 lb.) butter or margarine, held at room temperature for about 30 minutes (slightly soft, but still too firm to spread easily)
> Tart shapes (directions follow)
> Fillings (recipes follow)
> Water and sugar

Stir yeast into ¼ cup warm water and let stand 5 minutes. Add milk, egg, 3 tablespoons sugar, cardamom, and salt. Stir in 2 cups of flour. Beat with spoon until dough is smooth and elastic; beat in 2 more cups flour until well blended.

Coat board with several tablespoons flour. Place dough on board and pat some of the flour over surfaces; then knead until smooth and elastic;

takes about 10 minutes. Add more flour as required.

Cover and let rest about 5 minutes; then roll out dough to make a 16-inch square. Cut butter in thick slices, laying evenly onto one side of half the dough. Fold other half of dough over butter to encase it. Pinch edges together to seal. Roll out from the center, using firm but not heavy strokes to form a 12 by 16-inch rectangle. Fold ⅓ of the dough over center; then fold remaining ⅓ dough over the center. Wrap airtight and refrigerate 30 minutes.

On a floured board, roll dough to form a 16-inch square. Make 3 folds as before, folding sides over each other onto the center. Roll out again, rolling from folded edges to form the 16-inch square. Then again fold in thirds and chill as before. Repeat rolling, folding, and chilling procedure 2 more times.

After final chilling, shape tarts and fill according to the following directions; then brush with water and sprinkle with sugar *just* before baking.

(You can store unshaped pastry in the refrigerator overnight. Or freeze the shaped but unbaked pastries: place pastries in a single layer, wrap airtight, and freeze up to 1 month. Remove from freezer and let stand at room temperature about 30 minutes; then bake.)

Bake on ungreased rimmed baking sheets, slightly apart, in a 375° oven for about 25 minutes or until golden brown.

Serve pastries hot or cool slightly on wire racks and serve. To store cooled pastries, package airtight and freeze; reheat thawed pastries in a 350° oven for 10 minutes, uncovered. Makes about 3 dozen individual-sized pastries.

How to shape tarts (*Wienerbrød tœrte*). Roll out one recipe of Danish Pastry on a lightly-floured board to make a 24-inch square. Cut in

4-inch squares. Place about 1 teaspoon of any filling in the center of each square.

Fold to make any one of the three following shapes:

Envelope (*konvolute*). Fold one point over to within about 1 inch of the corner directly opposite.

Sheath (*skede*). Bring the points of 2 opposite corners to meet and overlap about ½ inch over the filling.

Packet (*pakke*). Bring the points of all four corners to the center, overlapping slightly.

Fillings. Each recipe makes about 1 cup; 2 cups fill one recipe's worth Danish Pastry. Keep cold, covered, until ready to use.

Apricot or Prune. Simmer 1 cup **dried apricots** or pitted dried prunes with 1 cup **water** and ½ cup **sugar,** covered, for about 20 minutes or until fruit is quite soft. Whirl smooth in a blender or rub through a wire strainer.

Almond. Blend 1 can or package (8 oz.) **almond paste** with 1 cup unsifted **powdered sugar** and 1 **egg** until smoothly mixed.

Prune and Almond Danish Pastry

If you haven't the time for the authentic Danish Pastry on page 57, frozen puff patty shells and a simple dried fruit and nut filling make showy and convincing substitutes.

> 1 package (10 oz.) frozen puff patty
>   shells
> 1 cup pitted dried prunes, cut in
>   halves
> 1 tablespoon granulated sugar
> 3 tablespoons water
> ¾ cup blanched almonds, finely
>   chopped
> ⅓ cup granulated sugar
> ½ teaspoon almond extract
>   Powdered Sugar Glaze (recipe
>   follows)

On a large rimmed baking sheet place the frozen patties (either side up) in 2 rows side by side, touching, and let thaw (about 20 minutes).

For the filling combine prunes, the 1 tablespoon sugar, and water in a small saucepan. Simmer, stirring occasionally, until liquid is mostly absorbed. Let cool.

Mix the almonds, the ⅓ cup sugar, and almond extract and set aside. Lightly brush surface of patty shells with flour (or dust a rolling pin stockinet cover with flour) and roll out dough to about 10 by 12 inches; the shape can be irregular.

Distribute about ⅔ of the almond mixture down the 12-inch length of the dough within 2 inches of the long sides. Line prunes up along each edge of the filling. Use a wide spatula to lift the edge of the pastry over the prunes to cover fruit. Strew the remaining almond mixture down the center.

Bake in a 450° oven for 18 to 20 minutes or until pastry is well browned; about 2 or 3 times, pat up fat extruded by baking pastry with paper towels to reduce the tendency to scorch or smoke.

Transfer hot pastry with wide spatulas to a serving tray and drizzle with the powdered sugar glaze. Serve hot or cold, cut in strips. Makes 8 servings.

Powdered Sugar Glaze. Mix ⅔ cup unsifted **powdered sugar** with about 3 teaspoons **water** to make an icing to drizzle.

From Finland: a Coffee Smörgåsbord

You eat seven baked sweets and sip at least four cups of coffee if you're having coffee the Finnish way. The occasion is a Coffee *Smörgåsbord*, the Finns' most engaging way to show hospitality.

SWEET YEAST BREAD

Choose either: Coffee Table Braids (see page 56) or Finnish Cardamom Wreath (see page 57)

UNICED CAKE

Choose either: Sandkaka (see page 61) or Snow Cake (see page 62)

FANCY CAKE

Princess Cake (see page 61) or Swedish Sour Cream Apple Cake (see page 63)

COOKIES

Choose four kinds: Orange Torte (see page 67) Gingerbread Pigs (see page 65) or Cinnamon Slices (see page 65) Finnish Ribbon Cakes (see page 66) or Nut-Crusted Logs (see page 65) Sandkakor (see page 65) or Swedish Spritz (see page 66)

COFFEE

with cream or cube sugar

You can entertain in the same manner, setting a lavish table with little effort. Make just one or two of the seven sweets and buy the rest from your baker.

Or to serve the authentic foods, set aside one grand day of baking before the party and prepare the breads, cakes, and cookies.

A Finnish Coffee Table can well serve a variety of occasions, evening or daytime: an informal gathering of the neighbors, a dessert party, a club or committee meeting. This coffee table is designed for a group of 12 to 18.

In Finland no two such tables are alike. Each homemaker serves her own combination of favorites to suit the occasion and her mood. Still, certain traditions are always observed that give almost an air of ritual:

1. Three main attractions appear on the coffee table: a sweet yeast bread, an uniced cake, and a fancy filled or decorated cake.

2. Altogether the table offers seven sweets. The main three are supplemented by four kinds of cookies.

3. The coffee table is served in three courses; the first consists of the sweet yeast bread and a cooky or two; the second is the un-iced cake, also taken with a few cookies; and the third is the fancy cake. (In Finland, it's considered a breach of etiquette if you don't sample a little of each course.)

4. Guests have at least one cup of coffee with each course. (Finnish coffee cups are about one-fourth smaller than ours). Difficult to master but also part of the ritual is drinking the last cup of coffee through a lump of sugar which you hold between your teeth.

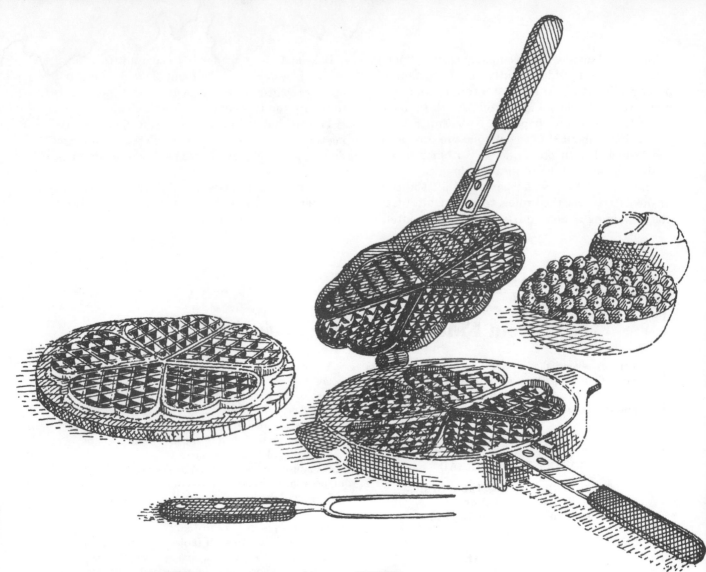

Sweet Treats

Fancy forms, traditional shapes, and some good standbys

Baking is the focus of the preceding chapter, and the oven is put to frequent use in this one, too. But there is method to our division; all of these foods have sweet aspects and belong in the role of a dessert or an occasional treat.

You'll discover a pretty variety of cakes and cookies. Some cakes are baked in molds, assembled in layers, or filled with fruit. Cookies take many forms; a collection of them arranged on a tray makes a handsome offering for tea-time or with after dinner coffee. Special tools that shape some traditional pastries are defined, and recipes for the pastries are included. Pancakes that make use of some of these tools—and many other pancakes that do not—are all intended for dessert service.

Fruits and puddings, some of which are flavored with fruit, follow, along with sauces that complement them and many other desserts.

Big Cakes, Little Cakes, and Cookies

Whether you need a delicious cake to serve unadorned, in thin slices, or a cake that is truly an artistic endeavor, a Scandinavian tradition here will fill the bill. Additionally, there are tarts—little cakes filled and to be filled.

A goodly number of the cookies start with a basic butter-rich dough, but each has a special shape or flavoring; you'll also find a sampling of other typical cookies. They suit lunch boxes, tea tables, and parties.

Sandkaka

Sandkaka, or Swedish Sand Cake, is made with rolled oats that are ground to a flour consistency in the blender. It has a coarse, compact texture, and a subtle lemon flavor.

1½ cups quick-cooking rolled oats
1 cup (½ lb.) soft butter or margarine
1¼ cups sugar
4 eggs
1 teaspoon grated lemon peel
2 tablespoons lemon juice
2 teaspoons vanilla
1¼ cups all-purpose flour, unsifted
  Fine dry bread crumbs

Whirl oats in a covered blender until ground to a flour; set aside. In the large bowl of your electric mixer blend butter with sugar smoothly. Beat in eggs, one at a time. Add lemon peel, lemon juice, and vanilla; stir to blend in. Gradually stir in the ground rolled oats and all-purpose flour until well mixed.

Butter and dust with fine dry bread crumbs a 6-cup-sized plain or fluted tube pan or a 5 by 9-inch loaf pan. Spoon in batter and smooth top. Bake in 325° oven for about 1 hour 10 minutes or until a wooden skewer, inserted, comes out clean. Cool in pan 10 minutes. Then invert onto serving dish to cool. Slice thinly. Makes 8 to 10 servings.

Princess Cake

Princess Cake (*Prinsesstårta*) is sponge cake layered with raspberry jam, vanilla custard, and whipped cream, and encased in a green-tinted marzipan wrapping.

Swedish bakers also make a tart size version of this lavish and popular dessert.

Day ahead preparation is recommended. The cake cuts and serves better, and a brief aging in the refrigerator blends flavors nicely.

1 can or package (8 oz.) almond paste
1 egg white
  About ½ cup unsifted powdered sugar
  Green food coloring
3 sponge cake layers, each 9-inch diameter (order from a bakery or make from your favorite recipe)
⅔ cup raspberry jam
  Vanilla Custard Filling (recipe follows)
1 cup whipping cream
1 teaspoon vanilla
¼ cup cinnamon red hot candies

Crumble almond paste into a bowl and mix in egg white and ½ cup powdered sugar. Add 3 drops green food coloring, or enough to tint a pale green. Knead with your hands and, if necessary, add 1 additional tablespoon powdered sugar to make the frosting fairly dry and not sticky. Form almond paste into a flat, round cake and place between two sheets of waxed paper that have been sprinkled lightly with powdered sugar. Use a rolling pin to roll out to form a circle about 15 inches in diameter (large enough to cover top and sides of filled cake). Chill until ready to use.

Spread the top of the first cake layer with ⅓ cup raspberry jam. Place second layer on top and spread with vanilla custard filling. Set the third cake layer on top; spread with the remaining ⅓ cup raspberry jam. Whip the cream with the vanilla until stiff, and carefully spread over the jam-covered top layer.

Remove marzipan from the refrigerator and peel off top sheet of waxed paper. Making sure the marzipan is centered on the cake, flop it over on to cake; peel off the other sheet of waxed paper. Press marzipan gently against the sides of the cake, pleating extra into folds; trim the bottom edge to make even.

(Continued on next page)

To decorate cake, work additional green food coloring into marzipan scraps making a darker hue; roll out between powdered sugar dusted sheets of waxed paper. Cut into leaf shapes with knife or cooky cutter. Place on top of cake; position cinnamon red hot candies to represent berries. Chill, covered, overnight. Serves 12 to 14.

Vanilla Custard Filling. In the top of a double boiler, mix together ¼ cup sugar, 1 teaspoon (part of a package) unflavored gelatin, and 2 teaspoons cornstarch. Stir in 1¼ cups milk. Cook over boiling water, stirring until thickened. Beat 2 egg yolks and stir in some of the hot milk mixture. Return to the top of the double boiler and place over simmering water; cook, stirring, 2 or 3 minutes longer. Remove from heat and stir in 1 teaspoon vanilla. Cool. Beat until stiff ½ cup whipping cream; fold into cool, but not set custard. Chill covered; use when firm enough to spread thickly.

Ring Tree Cake

Kransekake, or Ring Tree Cake (actually a tier of cookies), is a festival tradition in Norway. It's served at Christmas because of its gay tree shape, at weddings because of its impressive height, and at anniversary parties because of its many layers (as many rings as years to be celebrated).

First make the 26 paper patterns on which to shape the cooky rings. Use a compass to draw a circle 1 inch in diameter on brown or white wrapping paper (uncoated). Make each additional ring ¼ inch larger than the preceding one (the largest will be 7¼ inches in diameter). Number the patterns to keep them in order.

Beat together 2 cups (1 lb.) soft **butter** or margarine, 1 cup (8 oz. can or package) **almond paste,** 2 cups sifted **powdered sugar,** and 2 teaspoons **almond extract** until smooth. Beat 4 **egg yolks** in well. Sift **all-purpose flour,** measure 5 cups, and add gradually, mixing until very smooth.

Place paper patterns on ungreased baking sheets. With your hands, roll ½-inch diameter strands of dough and fit against inside edges of paper patterns; piece coils as needed (or force dough through a pastry bag or cooky press with a ½-inch plain tip). Bake in 350° oven for 15 to 20 minutes or until delicately browned. Cool on baking sheet; free rings from paper with a long, thin spatula or knife.

To assemble cake, place largest ring on a flat plate, top with next largest ring; continue stacking rings in order of the next smaller until you've used all layers. Decorate if you like, with purchased **marzipan fruits;** stick with small wooden picks and slide picks between layers to hold in place. Lift off rings and break into portions to serve. Serves 30 to 35.

Snow Cake

Make effective use of leftover egg whites in snow cake. It doesn't rise while baking, and has a fine, springy, even texture.

> 1 cup egg whites (about 8 whites)
> About 1 cup granulated sugar
> ¼ teaspoon salt
> 1 teaspoon vanilla
> 1 cup all-purpose flour
> 1 teaspoon baking powder
> ½ cup (¼ lb.) butter or margarine, melted and cooked
> Powdered sugar

In a large bowl of your electric mixer whip the egg whites until foamy. Then at highest speed, gradually add 1 cup granulated sugar and beat until mixture will stand in stiff, but not dry, peaks; then stir in the salt and vanilla.

Sift flour and measure. Then sift again with baking powder into the egg whites, folding until blended. Fold in butter until evenly mixed. Pour batter into a well-greased and granulated sugar-dusted, 2-quart-size, fancy or plain tube pan. Bake in 350° oven for 1 hour or until cake bounces back when touched lightly in the center. Let stand 10 minutes; then invert from pan onto a wire rack to cool. Dust well with powdered sugar and cut in thin slices to serve. Makes 9 to 12 servings.

Swedish Sour Cream Apple Cake

To make this old-fashioned baked fruit-custard cake, you first steam the apples with butter and sugar.

- 2 tablespoons butter or margarine
- 6 cups peeled, cored, and thinly sliced Golden Delicious apples
- ⅔ cup sugar
- 1½ tablespoons *each* cornstarch and water
- 6 eggs
- 2 cups (1 pt.) sour cream
- 2 teaspoons vanilla
  Zwieback Crust (directions follow)

Melt butter in a wide frying pan and add apples and sugar. Cover and cook over moderate heat for about 10 minutes, stirring frequently, until apples just start to soften. Blend cornstarch with water and pour into apples; cook, stirring gently, until thickened. Remove from heat. Beat eggs with sour cream and vanilla; mix with apples. Pour mixture into cheesecake pan lined with Zwieback Crust.

Bake in a 325° oven for 35 minutes or until center of cake jiggles but looks set when pan is gently shaken.

Chill, remove pan rim, and cut in wedges to serve. Makes 9 to 12 servings.

Zwieback Crust. Finely crush 1 package (6 oz.) **zwieback.** In a 9-inch cheesecake pan (with removable sides) mix crumbs with 2 tablespoons **sugar,** 1 teaspoon **ground cinnamon,** and ¼ cup soft **butter** or margarine. Press evenly over bottom and about 2 inches up the side of pan.

Applecake

This is not a cake in our sense of the word; it's a combination of cooked apples and flavorful crumbs, with embellishments such as cream, tart jelly, or jam. It may be served with or without cooking.

Each of the four Scandinavian countries claims various styles of applecake, but usually it depends upon what the cook has on hand. We give you a few options, too.

Coarsely crush 1 package (6 oz.) **zwieback.** Melt 6 tablespoons **butter** or margarine in a wide frying pan over moderate heat; add crumbs, ½ cup sugar, and 2 teaspoons **ground cinnamon.** Stir until crumbs give off a nice toasty aroma; set aside.

Peel and slice 8 large (about 4 lbs.) tart **apples.** Melt 2 tablespoons butter or margarine in a wide frying pan; add 1 tablespoon sugar, 1 tablespoon **lemon juice,** and the apples. Cover and cook over medium heat, turning frequently with a wide spatula until fruit is tender when pierced; takes about 10 minutes.

In a 9-inch square pan (or other shallow pan of equivilent area) layer cooked apples and crumbs, making 2 or 3 layers of each, starting with apples and ending with crumbs. Cover and chill at least 6 hours or overnight.

If desired, you can unmold the cake in this fashion: cover pan with a serving dish; hold together, invert, and remove pan.

Beat 1 cup **whipping cream** until it holds soft peaks. Frost top (and sides, if unmolded) of cake with cream. Sprinkle with about ⅓ cup toasted sliced **almonds** and dot (if desired) with spoonfuls (about ½ cup total) **red currant jelly.** Spoon into dessert dishes to serve. Makes 8 to 10 servings.

Baked Applecake. Follow directions for **Applecake** (see above), but instead of using zwieback, coarsely crush enough **oatmeal cookies** (about a 12 oz. package) to make 3½ cups crumbs. Layer crumbs and **apples** in pan, starting and ending with crumbs. Top with ½ cup chopped **almonds** (omit sliced almonds). Bake, uncovered, in a 375° oven for about 25 minutes or until heated through. Serve hot, warm, or cold (chill, covered, overnight, if more convenient). Serve **whipping cream** to pour over individual servings; omit jelly.

Cream-puff Cake Strips

Serve plain or accompany with berries and whipped cream to spoon onto individual portions.

- 1 cup (½ lb.) butter or margarine
- 2 cups all-purpose flour, unsifted
  Water
- 4 eggs
- ½ teaspoon almond extract
- 1 cup unsifted powdered sugar
- 2 tablespoons milk
- ⅓ cup sliced or slivered toasted almonds

Cut half the butter in small pieces and mix with 1 cup of the flour. Rub with fingers until evenly mixed. Stir in 2 tablespoons water until dough holds together. Divide equally. Pat each portion out evenly on ungreased baking sheet to form two strips each 4 by 10 inches (spacing apart).

Bring 1 cup water and remaining ½ cup butter, cut in pieces, to a boil. Dump in remaining 1 cup flour, remove from heat, and beat to blend. Add eggs, one at a time, beating well after each addition. Mix in extract. Spread mixture equally and evenly over both pastry strips. Bake in a 350° oven for 1 hour or until well browned. Leave on baking pan while cooling.

Smoothly blend sugar and milk; spread on top of slightly warm pastries; sprinkle with nuts. Serve warm or cold. Makes 2 strips, each serving 6.

Mazarin

One of the most popular pastries in Stockholm, this almond paste-based tart is served automatically when you ask for a pastry but don't specify which kind. You can make individual tarts or a single large one.

    Mazarin Pastry (directions follow)
 1 **can or package (8 oz. or ¾ cup)**
       almond paste
 2 **tablespoons** *each* **granulated sugar**
       and all-purpose flour
 2 **eggs**
 1 **egg white**
 ¼ **teaspoon almond extract**
 1 **cup unsifted powdered sugar**
 2 **tablespoons milk**

Divide pastry in 8 equal portions and press each portion evenly over bottom and sides of ½-cup size plain or fluted tart pans.

Break almond paste into small pieces; then, with a mixer or spoon, mix evenly with granulated sugar and flour. Add eggs, one at a time, and egg white, blending smoothly. Stir in the almond extract.

Spoon an equal portion of the mixture into each of the prepared mazarin pastry shells (for easier handling, set all the tart pans on a baking sheet).

Bake in a 325° oven for about 30 minutes or until pastries are richly browned on top. Let cool about 5 minutes. Blend powdered sugar smoothly with milk; spoon an equal portion of this mixture onto each tart, then spread to coat surfaces.

Let cool; with a knife tip to help, ease tarts from pans. Serve, or store as long as 2 days in an airtight container; wrap airtight and freeze for longer storage. Makes 8 individual tarts.

Mazarin Pastry. Stir together 5 tablespoons **sugar** and 1½ cups unsifted **all-purpose flour.** Cut ½ cup (¼ lb.) **butter** or margarine in small pieces and mix with flour; rub mixture with your fingers until evenly mixed. With a fork stir in 1 **egg yolk** then compress mixture with your hands until it holds together.

Mazarin Tart. Follow directions for making **Mazarin** (see this page) but use all the pastry to line a 9-inch cheesecake pan or cake pan with removable bottom, pressing dough up about 1 inch on pan sides. Pour all the filling into the pan. Bake in a 325° oven for about 1 hour and 10 minutes or until top is golden brown. Glaze as directed. When cool, remove pan rim. Cut in wedges. Makes 8 to 10 servings.

Almond Tarts

Fill with fruit and top with sweetened whipped cream at serving time. For each tart use 2 or 3 tablespoons fresh or frozen fruit or canned pie filling (blueberry or cherry), or 2 or 3 teaspoons jam or jelly.

Whirl ⅓ cup unblanched whole **almonds** in a covered blender until finely ground. Mix with 2½ cups unsifted **all-purpose flour** and ½ cup **sugar.** Add 1 cup (½ lb.) **butter** or margarine; rub with your fingers until evenly mixed.

With a fork, stir in 1 **egg** to thoroughly blend. Shape dough into a compact ball; then divide into 2-tablespoon-size portions. Press each portion evenly over bottom and sides of ⅓-cup-size tart pans (use less dough for smaller pans, more for larger pans). Place pans on a baking sheet. Bake in a 325° oven for 25 to 30 minutes or until brown.

Let cool on wire racks; then invert to release from pans. Store airtight; keep 3 or 4 days at room temperature or freeze for longer storage. Makes about 2 dozen tarts; allow 1 or 2 per serving.

Basic Cooky Dough

One rich dough that you vary in flavor and by shaping is the starting point for an impressive number of traditional cookies. And because of their richness, the cookies are best stored in the freezer if you do not plan to serve them within several days.

Beat until smoothly blended 1 cup (½ lb.) soft

butter or margarine with ½ cup **sugar.** Stir in 1 **egg yolk,** ¼ teaspoon **salt,** and 3 cups unsifted **all-purpose flour;** blend well. Flavor, shape, and bake according to following directions. Cool on wire racks. Store airtight 2 or 3 days at room temperature or freeze for longer storage.

Cut-out Cookies. Follow **Basic Cooky Dough** (see opposite page) recipe adding 1 **whole egg** instead of the yolk, and mixing in 1 teaspoon **vanilla.** Roll out on a lightly floured board or pastry cloth to ⅛-inch thickness. Cut with floured cutters into decorative shapes. Place slightly apart on lightly greased baking sheets. Bake in a 350° oven for about 12 to 15 minutes or until cookies are very lightly browned. Makes about 5½ dozen cookies about 2 inches in diameter.

Nut-crusted Logs. Shape **Basic Cooky Dough** (see opposite page) into ½-inch-thick ropes; cut in 2-inch lengths. Beat 1 **egg** in a shallow pan. Roll each length in egg, lifting to drain; then roll ropes in a mixture of ¼ cup finely chopped or ground **almonds** and 2 tablespoons **sugar.** Place cookies slightly apart on a greased baking sheet. Bake in a 350° oven for about 15 minutes or until very lightly browned. Makes about 4 dozen.

Cinnamon Slices. Mix 1 teaspoon **vanilla** into the **Basic Cooky Dough** (see opposite page) with the **egg yolk.** Shape into logs about 1 to 1¼-inch diameter. Roll in a mixture of ¼ cup **sugar** and 1 tablespoon **ground cinnamon,** pressing lightly to make coating stick. Wrap and chill. Cut dough in ⅛-inch-thick slices and place slightly apart on lightly ungreased baking sheets. Brush tops with 1 beaten **egg;** then sprinkle with sugar and press 1 blanched **almond** or 2 pieces sliced almond on the center of each. Bake in a 350° oven for 12 to 15 minutes or until firm but still quite pale. Makes about 15 dozen.

Rich Cut-out Cookies. Make **Basic Cooky Dough** (see opposite page), reducing flour to 2 cups. Chill dough. Roll out on a floured board or pastry cloth to about ⅛-inch thickness. Cut with floured cutters into decorative shapes. Place slightly apart on ungreased baking sheets. Bake in a 350° oven for about 12 to 15 minutes or until pale gold or lightly browned. Makes about 5 dozen cookies 2 inches in diameter.

Jam-filled Rich Cut-out Cookies. Make **Rich Cut-out Cookies** (see above), cutting each shape in pairs. Bake as directed and cool. Spread the tops of half the cookies with this mixture: 1 cup sifted

powdered sugar blended smoothly with 1 tablespoon **milk.** Spread **raspberry jam** on top each of the remaining cookies (you'll need about ½ cup total) and set a glazed cooky of the same shape on top. Decorate tops with a dot of the jam, if you like. Makes about 2½ dozen filled cookies about 2 inches in diameter.

Gingerbread Pigs. Prepare **Basic Cooky Dough** (see opposite page), adding ¼ cup **dark molasses,** 2 teaspoons *each* ground cinnamon and **ground cardamom,** 1 teaspoon **ground ginger,** ½ teaspoon **ground nutmeg,** and ⅛ teaspoon **pepper,** along with sugar. Chill dough if too soft to roll easily.

Roll out ⅛ inch thick on floured board or pastry cloth and cut with flour-dusted, pig-shaped cutter (or any fancy cooky cutter). Place slightly apart on ungreased baking sheets. Bake in a 350° oven for about 10 minutes or until firm to touch and slightly darker at edges. If desired, apply decorations when cool, using white decorating icing in tube or aerosol can forced through a narrow plain tip. Makes about 3 dozen, 3 to 4-inch pigs.

Swedish Almond Cookies. Make **Basic Cooky Dough** (see opposite page), increasing the **sugar** to 1 cup and adding ¼ teaspoon **almond extract** and 1 **whole egg** instead of the egg yolk. Decrease the **flour** to 2 cups and add 1 cup ground **almonds** with the flour. Shape dough in about 1-inch-diameter balls. Place about an inch apart on ungreased baking sheets. Flatten each with a floured fork. Bake in a 350° oven for 15 to 18 minutes or until golden. Makes about 5½ dozen.

Sandkakor. Make **Basic Cooky Dough** (see opposite page), increasing **sugar** to ⅔ cup, adding ½ teaspoon **ground cardamom,** and ¼ teaspoon **soda** with the sugar, and decreasing **flour** to 2 cups.

Shape dough in about 1-inch balls. Place slightly apart on ungreased baking sheets. Bake in a 350°

oven for about 15 to 18 minutes or until golden. Makes about 4 dozen.

Finnish Ribbon Cakes. Make **Basic Cooky Dough** (see page 64), decreasing the **flour** to 2½ cups. Shape in ropes about ½ inch in diameter. Place ropes the length of an ungreased baking sheet, keeping ropes about 2 inches apart. With the side of your little finger, press a long groove down the length of each strand. Bake in a 375° oven for 10 minutes.

Remove cookies from oven and spoon **jam** or jelly into the groove (takes about 6 tablespoons). Return to oven for about 5 to 10 minutes more or until dough is firm to touch and light golden in color. While hot, brush with a glaze of ½ cup unsifted **powdered sugar** blended with 2 tablespoons **water** or milk. Cut logs at about a 45° angle in 1-inch lengths. Cool briefly on baking sheets before transferring to wire racks. Makes about 9 dozen.

Swedish Spritz. Make **Basic Cooky Dough** (see page 64), increasing the **sugar** to ¾ cup, the **egg yolks** to 3, and add 1 **whole egg.** Add along with the sugar ½ teaspoon **baking powder,** 1 teaspoon **vanilla,** and ¼ teaspoon **almond extract.** Decrease **flour** to 2½ cups.

Place dough in a cooky press with ridged extrusion plate or rosette tip. Force dough onto ungreased baking sheets, forming rings about 2 inches across. Bake in a 350° oven for 10 to 15 minutes or until a light golden color. Makes about 5 dozen.

Norwegian Kringle or Bowknot Cookies. Make **Basic Cooky Dough** (see page 64), increasing **sugar** to 1 cup and adding with it 2 hard-cooked **egg yolks,** finely mashed, and 1 **whole egg.**

Pinch off 1-inch balls of dough and roll each to form a 6-inch-long strand. Form each strand into a ring or pretzel shape on greased baking sheets, spacing slightly apart. Brush shaped dough with 1 **egg white,** beaten until frothy; then sprinkle with granulated **sugar** or coarsely crushed sugar cubes.

Bake in a 350° oven for 12 to 15 minutes or until pale golden brown. Makes about 4½ dozen.

Oatmeal Crisps

These crisp cookies spread out as they bake.

Blend smoothly 1 cup (½ lb.) soft **butter** or margarine, 1½ cups **sugar,** and 2 teaspoons **soda.** Add 1 **egg** and beat well. Stir 2 cups unsifted **all-pur-**

pose flour into butter mixture with 1¼ cups **regular rolled oats** and 1 cup **raisins.** Mix until blended. Drop by rounded teaspoonfuls about 1½ inches apart onto well greased baking sheets, spacing about 2 inches apart.

Bake in a 375° oven for 10 to 15 minutes or until lightly browned. Let stand a few minutes; then remove from baking sheets and cool on wire racks. Store airtight up to a week. Freeze for longer storage. Makes about 8 dozen.

Rye Cookies

(*Ruiskakut*)

Rye cookies are a Christmas tradition in Finland. They are rounds with slightly off-center holes cut in them.

> 1 **cup rye flour**
> ½ **cup all-purpose flour, unsifted**
> ¼ **teaspoon salt**
> ½ **cup sugar**
> ½ **cup (¼ lb.) butter or margarine, cut in pieces**
> 4 **to 5 tablespoons milk**

Stir the flours together with salt and sugar in a mixing bowl. Add butter and rub with your fingers until mixture resembles fine crumbs. Add the milk, 1 tablespoon at a time, stirring with a fork until a stiff dough is formed. Gather together and press into a ball. Chill. Then roll a portion at a time on a floured board or pastry cloth to about ⅛-inch thickness. Cut out rounds with a 2-inch cooky cutter. Using a tiny round cutter (½-inch diameter—you can use the cap from a food coloring or flavoring bottle), cut a hole slightly off center. Prick each cooky several times with a fork and place on lightly greased baking sheets, slightly apart. Bake in a 375° oven for 8 to 10 minutes or until cookies are firm when touched. Cool on wire racks. Store airtight at room temperature for 2 or 3 days; freeze for longer storage. Makes about 2 dozen.

Desert Sand Cookies

Browned butter and an intriguing texture help earn these cookies their name.

Melt ½ cup (¼ lb.) **butter** or margarine over medium heat until butter begins to turn brown.

Transfer to a deep bowl and beat with a rotary mixer until lukewarm. Beat in ¾ cup **sugar** gradually until mixture is pale and fluffy; stir in 1 teaspoon **vanilla,** 1 teaspoon **baking powder,** and 1 cup unsifted **all-purpose flour.** Shape dough into 1-inch balls. Place slightly apart on ungreased baking sheets. Bake in a 350° oven for about 18 minutes or until lightly browned. Cool on pans. Store airtight at room temperature for 2 or 3 days; freeze for longer storage. Makes about 3 dozen.

Norwegian Oatmeal Lace Cookies

To curl these cookies, drape them over a horizontal broomstick handle covered with foil.

    ½ **cup (¼ lb.) butter or margarine**
    1½ **cups regular rolled oats**
    1 **egg**
    ⅔ **cup sugar**
    1 **teaspoon baking powder**
    1 **tablespoon all-purpose flour**

Melt the butter in a small saucepan and stir in the oatmeal. Beat egg until foamy with the sugar. Mix together the baking powder and flour and stir into the egg mixture along with the oatmeal mixture. Drop batter, 1 level tablespoonful at a time, onto greased and floured baking sheets, 2 to 3 inches apart.

Bake in a 375° oven for 10 minutes or until golden brown. Place baking sheets on wire racks to cool about 1 minute (cookies should still be hot and flexible but cooled until firm enough to move). Quickly lift cookies with a spatula; drape over foil-covered broom handle; press gently into saddle shape. (If cookies harden and stick to pan, return to oven until softened). When cool, lift off broomstick. Store airtight at room temperature 2 or 3 days; freeze for longer storage. Makes about 2 dozen.

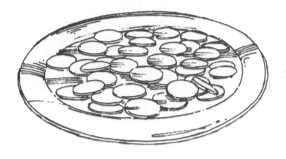

Orange Torte

(*Appelsiinitortu*)

Bake this long, slender, log-shaped torte filled with ground almonds and sugar; then cut it into thin slices to make cookies.

Cut ½ cup (¼ lb.) **butter** or margarine into pieces; rub into 1½ cups unsifted **all-purpose flour** and ¼ cup **sugar** until particles are fine. Stir in 1 **egg yolk.** Gather the crumbly mixture together to form a ball; squeeze between your palms until the warmth of your hands makes a smooth dough. On a lightly floured board, roll dough out into a rectangle 5 by 10 inches.

Mix together 2 teaspoons slightly beaten **egg white,** 1 cup ground **almonds,** and ¾ cup sugar. Turn mixture onto clean board; press together firmly to form a log about 8 inches long; place lengthwise down middle of dough rectangle. Bring up the two long sides of dough overlapping edges slightly to enclose the filling; press to seal and make a smooth seam. Pinch ends together to seal. Carefully lift filled roll onto a lightly greased baking sheet, placing seam side down. Bake in a hot oven (400°) for 15 minutes or until golden. Cool on baking sheet. When cool, drizzle top of torte with icing made by mixing ¼ cup unsifted **powdered sugar** and about 1 tablespoon **orange juice.** Decorate with strips of **candied orange peel** and **glacéed cherries.** At serving time, cut into thin slices. Makes about 18 pieces.

Swedish Ginger Cookies

(*Pepparkakor*)

Very spicy, very thin, and very crisp ginger cookies.

    ⅔ **cup butter or margarine**
    ⅓ **cup *each* granulated sugar and**
          firmly packed brown sugar
    2 **tablespoons dark corn syrup**
    2 **teaspoons *each* ground ginger and**
          ground cloves
    1 **tablespoon ground cinnamon**
    2 **teaspoons soda**
    ¼ **cup water**
    2½ **cups all-purpose flour, unsifted**

Combine the butter, sugars, and corn syrup in a saucepan. Stir over low heat until the butter is melted. Remove from heat, blend in ginger, cloves, and cinnamon, and cool slightly. Mix soda with water then add to dough. Stir in the flour and mix until well blended. Dough will be quite soft. Wrap well and chill.

Roll portions of chilled dough on a floured board or pastry cloth to about 1/16-inch thickness. Cut out with floured cooky cutters and place slightly apart on ungreased baking sheets. Bake in a 325° oven for about 6 to 10 minutes or until slightly darker brown. Cool on pans. Store airtight 4 or 5 days at room temperature; freeze for longer storage. Reroll scraps of dough until all is used. Makes about 10 dozen 2-inch cookies.

To decorate, use your favorite decorating icing or this durable Royal Icing: in small bowl of electric mixer, beat at high speed 1 **egg white** with ⅛ teaspoon **cream of tartar** and dash of **salt** for 1 minute. Add 2 cups sifted **powdered sugar.** Beat slowly until blended; then beat at high speed until very stiff (3 to 5 minutes). Keep tightly covered in refrigerator.

Press icing through decorating tube with plain tip, making swirls and outline designs on cookies. Allow frosting to dry before storing cookies.

Gingerbread Cooky Houses to Build and to Break

First roll the spicy gingerbread dough right onto the baking sheet: one pan yields one house; the recipe yields three. Then cut house sections when the cooky is partially baked to assure precise, easily fit edges; eat remaining scraps.

Thoroughly blend 1⅓ cups soft **butter** or margarine, 1½ cups firmly packed **brown sugar,** 2 tablespoons **ground cinnamon,** 4 teaspoons **ground ginger,** 1 tablespoon *each* **ground cloves** and **soda.** Add ½ cup **water** and 5 cups unsifted, **all-purpose flour** and mix well. Divide dough into 3 equal portions. With a well floured rolling pin (or one with a floured stockinet cover), roll each portion in an even layer on an ungreased 12 by 15-inch baking sheet without sides; cover pan completely. With a wide spatula, push dough about ⅜ inch back from rimless edges; press down the ridge that forms to make level.

Bake one cooky at a time in a 300° oven; after 15 minutes remove the cooky and quickly arrange

pattern. Return at once to the oven and continue baking 15 to 25 minutes more or until cooky feels firm to touch (time varies according to how much the cooky cooled while cutting).

Repeat procedure for each cooky house. Transfer hot cookies to wire racks to cool; package airtight until ready to decorate. Eat within 2 weeks if held at room temperature; freeze for longer storage. Makes 3 cooky houses.

To decorate cooky houses, apply purchased **icing** for decorating (in tubes or aerosol cans) to flat sections and let dry at least 30 minutes.

To assemble each cooky house, apply icing to bottom and side edges of house front, back, and walls; fit these pieces together on a firm surface, such as a small cutting board. Let stand a few minutes for icing to set; then apply icing to top edges. Set roof sections in place. Apply icing to sides and bottoms of chimney pieces and set in place against roof ridge.

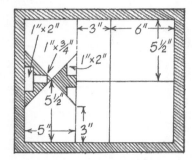

on it the pattern (cut from posterboard or heavy paper) as shown above. Cut around each piece with a sharp knife but leave all on pan; remove

Position *decorated cooky roof on icing-coated house edges; you can fill the house with goodies.*

Pastries with Special Shapes

The cooking tools on page 76 give these foods their unique form, and since these tools are relatively inexpensive and often found even in the housewares sections of large department stores, you might like to add them to your own collection of culinary equipment.

The cooky "bakes" over direct heat, flattened to a paper-thin disc by the cooky iron. The pancakes become balls by continuing attention as they, too, "bake" over direct heat. (Another utensil, the platte pan, makes a different pancake—see page 76). You can make the waffles in any waffle baker, but the heart shape is a pretty tradition. Rosette irons for making the thin fried pastries are available with even more variations in shapes and designs than could be found a few years ago.

Krumkake

Thin, golden *Krumkake* cookies that can be served flat or rolled and filled are baked in an iron either 5 or 6 inches in diameter.

Beat 3 **eggs** with ½ cup **sugar,** 6 tablespoons melted **butter** or margarine, ½ teaspoon *each* **lemon extract** and **ground cardamom** (optional). Blend in ⅔ cup unsifted **all-purpose flour** until smooth.

To bake a cooky, place iron directly over medium-high heat. Alternately heat both sides of the iron until water dripped inside sizzles. Open and brush lightly with melted butter. For each cooky, spoon about 1 tablespoon batter into center of a buttered 5-inch iron (about 1½ tablespoons in 6-inch iron); close and squeeze handles together. Turn iron and scrape off any batter that flows out. Bake, turning about every 20 seconds, until cooky is light golden brown; open often to check doneness. Quickly lift out cooky with a fork or spatula; return iron to heat. Let the cooky cool flat on wire racks or shape in a cone while still hot and pliable; then cool. Store in airtight containers for a week at room temperature; freeze for longer storage. Serve plain or fill just before serving with **whipped cream.** Makes about 1½ dozen.

Danish Pancake Balls

(*Aebleskiver*)

The tender, ball-shaped cakes that the Danes call *aebleskiver* (aw-bluh skeever) take their shape from the pan in which they bake on top of the range. It's technique, though, that makes *aebleskiver* round. You keep lifting and turning the baked section of the ball until eventually it seals itself. Eat hot for dessert or breakfast.

1¼ cups all-purpose flour
½ teaspoon salt
2¼ teaspoons baking powder
2 tablespoons sugar
½ teaspoon ground cardamom or ground cinnamon
1 egg, beaten
1 cup milk
About 6 tablespoons butter or margarine, melted and cooled
Powdered sugar
Strawberry jam, raspberry jam, or other preserves

Sift flour before measuring; then sift again into a bowl with the salt, baking powder, sugar, and cardamom. Combine egg, milk, and 2 tablespoons of the butter; add to flour mixture and stir until blended and smooth.

Place a seasoned *aebleskiver* pan over medium-low heat until water sprinkled in pan sizzles. Brush each cup lightly with melted butter; then fill each about ¾ full with batter. In about 30 seconds a thin shell will form on the bottom of each pancake ball. Stick a slender skewer into baked portion and gently pull shell almost halfway up so unbaked batter flows out.

Continue to rotate each pancake ball about every 30 seconds as the shell begins to set, pulling up the baked shell to let remaining batter flow out into pan. After about four turns, the ball should be almost formed and you can turn it upside down to seal. Continue baking, rotating the balls frequently to make them an even golden brown and until a wooden skewer inserted in the center comes out clean. Lift balls with skewer from pan as baked. Serve immediately or keep warm up to 30 minutes in a bun warmer or cloth-lined basket on an electric warming tray. Dust with powdered sugar, break each ball in half, fill with jam, and eat out of hand. Makes 12 to 15 pancakes.

Rosettes

Rosettes, a Christmas tradition in Scandinavia, are usually served like cookies with coffee, but some are filled with flavored whipped cream for desserts.

Beat together until well mixed (but not foamy) 2 **eggs**, 2 teaspoons **sugar**, ¼ teaspoon **salt**, 1 cup **milk**, and 3 teaspoons **lemon extract**. Sift **all-purpose flour**, measure 1 cup, and beat into liquid ingredients until smooth (batter should be like thick cream).

Have batter in a container just wide enough to permit easy dipping with irons. Also choose a deep saucepan of similar dimensions. Place irons in a saucepan, add about 1½ inches **salad oil**, and heat to 370°.

Touch hot iron quickly to paper towel to absorb excess oil; then dip at once in the batter (don't let batter come over top edge of iron or it will be hard to remove) and immerse quickly into fat for about 30 seconds or until pastry is golden brown. Remove from fat and loosen Rosettes with fork; drain on absorbent paper.

Store the pastries in airtight container 2 or 3 days at room temperature; freeze for longer storage. Sprinkle with **powdered sugar** before serving. Makes about 5 dozen.

Crisp Heart-shaped Waffles

This batter literally explodes in the iron. Baking powder helps these wonderfully crisp and fragile waffles hold their shape.

Beat together 1¼ cups unsifted **all-purpose flour** and ¾ cup **water** until smooth. Stir in ¼ cup **whipping cream**, 2 tablespoons **sugar**, 1½ teaspoons **vanilla**, 2¼ teaspoons **baking powder**, and ⅛ teaspoon **salt**. Beat 1 cup **whipping cream** until stiff; then fold into the batter. Place a seasoned, heart-shaped waffle iron on medium-low heat, turning it over until water dripped inside sizzles (or preheat an electric waffle iron as manufacturer directs).

Open iron and spoon about ⅓ cup batter into heart-shaped iron (or use amount recommended for grids of other shapes and bake as manufacturer directs). Close heart iron, squeezing handles gently; then turn iron over about every 30 seconds or until waffle is golden brown (about 4 minutes); open iron often to check doneness. Transfer waffles to a wire rack. Serve warm or cool completely; then package airtight. Store at room temperature 3 or 4 days or freeze for longer storage. Eat plain, like a cooky, or topped with **whipped cream** and **sweetened berries**. Makes 8 to 10 whole waffles.

Dessert Pancakes

These thin pancakes, small or large, are very much like French *crêpes*, whereas the puffy oven pancakes have a variety of qualities. They may be brown and voluminous like Yorkshire pudding or thick and velvety textured preparations that combine some of the delicious qualities of omelets, sweet soufflés, and baked custards. All these are served when freshly made.

Toppings or accompaniments are suggested with each recipe, but keep in mind that fresh fruits of the season are also complimentary, and add yet additional dimensions to these desserts.

Tiny Swedish Pancakes

(*Tunna Pannkakor*)

These tender little pancakes are usually served with tart lingonberry preserves. They may be dessert (perhaps after split pea soup or some other hearty soup) or served with pork (or crisp bacon) as a main dish combination for breakfast or supper. You can also make these pancakes in a *crêpe* or omelet pan, using enough batter each time to coat the pan bottom.

½ cup all-purpose flour, unsifted
1 tablespoon granulated sugar
½ teaspoon salt
1 cup half and half (light cream) or milk
2½ tablespoons water
2 eggs, slightly beaten
   Melted butter
   Tart jelly and powdered sugar

Mix flour, sugar, and salt in a bowl. Add cream, water, and eggs and beat until smooth.

Place seasoned Swedish pancake iron over medium heat until hot enough to make a drop of water dance. Brush each pancake cup with melted butter (do this each time). Pour just enough batter (about 2 teaspoons) into each cup to barely coat the bottom (tilt pan to distribute).

Bake until surface of each cake looks dry. Then turn with a thin-bladed knife and continue cooking until lightly browned on the bottom. Stack and keep warm until all are cooked. (Or let cool; reheat, covered, in a 350° oven for 10 to 15 minutes.) Serve cakes in stacks, folded, or rolled; put a dot of jelly on each pancake, if desired. Dust cakes with powdered sugar and serve hot. Makes about 60 cakes; allow 6 or 8 for a dessert serving or 8 to 10 for a side dish serving.

Swedish Pancakes

Big, thin, round pancakes are made in a regular frying pan. Serve them following Swedish Pea Soup (see page 21) or as dessert for any meal, folded around fruit or topped with a sauce.

In a bowl stir together 1½ cups unsifted **all-purpose flour**, ¼ teaspoon **salt**, ¼ cup **sugar,** and 1 teaspoon **baking powder.** Beat 6 **eggs** lightly; mix into flour. Gradually add 4 cups **milk**; blend smooth. Stir in ¼ cup melted **butter** or margarine.

To make each pancake, melt ½ teaspoon butter or margarine in a 10 or 11-inch flat-bottom frying pan (measured across base) over medium to medium-high heat. Pour in 3 tablespoons of the batter all at once, tilting pan to coat bottom evenly.

When pancake is dry on top, run a long-bladed spatula around the edge to make sure it is free. To turn, lift pan, tipping to let pancake roll out and fall across the length of the spatula. Then lay the uncooked side of pancake down into pan, guiding in place with spatula. Let cook until lightly browned on the underside. Turn out onto a flat pan. Repeat to make each pancake, stacking them.

Fold each pancake in half. Arrange in several stacks on an oven-proof serving platter. Cover with foil. Chill as long as 2 or 3 days (or wrap airtight and freeze; let thaw to use). To reheat, place platter in a 300° oven for 30 minutes.

Serve with **whipped cream** to spoon onto hot pancakes, topping with dabs of **tart preserves,** jam, or jelly (lingonberry, boysenberry, raspberry); you can fold pancakes over cream, if you like. You'll need about 1½ cups whipping cream, beaten stiff and sweetened to taste, and about 1½ cups jelly. Makes about 3 dozen or 12 to 14 servings.

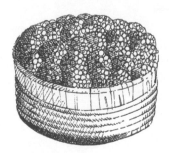

Apricot Pannukakku

Apricot *Pannukakku,* a Finnish oven pancake, must be served warm, so assemble the three fresh-from-the-oven layers at the last minute. You can prepare the batter several hours in advance and refrigerate it.

To facilitate the assembling of this warm, fragile dessert, turn layers out onto a buttered plate. Then slip them into place on the serving dish.

　½　cup (¼ lb.) butter or margarine
　1　cup all-purpose flour, unsifted
　4　cups milk
　7　eggs
　1½　cups apricot jam
　1　cup whipping cream
　5　tablespoons powdered sugar

In a 2 to 3-quart saucepan, melt butter and blend in flour. Gradually blend in milk and cook over direct heat, stirring, until boiling and thickened. Cool mixture to lukewarm; beat in eggs, one at a time. Pour equally into three greased 9-inch cake pans (ones with removable bottoms are best, if you have them). Bake in a 400° oven for about 30 minutes or until the layers are puffed and golden brown.

Meanwhile, melt jam in a saucepan over low heat and keep warm. Whip the cream until stiff with 1 tablespoon powdered sugar.

Remove all three layers of *pannukakku* from the oven. Gently turn out one layer at a time onto a heavily buttered plate. Then carefully slide the pancake onto a serving platter; spoon half of the warm jam evenly over the top. Turn out the second layer on the buttered plate. Slide it onto the jam-topped first layer and spoon remaining warm jam over it. Turn out the third layer in the same manner and slide it onto second layer. Sift the ¼ cup powdered sugar evenly over the top. Serve immediately by cutting in wedges and topping each wedge with the sweetened whipped cream (or pass the whipped cream at the table). Makes 8 servings.

Oven Pancake

Since this pancake is a sweet version of the same basic mixture as used to make popovers or Yorkshire pudding, it puffs up in the oven. Present it promptly, for it settles when cool.

In a blender container, combine 1 cup **milk**, ⅔ cup unsifted **all-purpose flour**, 2 tablespoons **sugar**, ½ teaspoon **salt**, 2 **eggs**, ½ teaspoon **grated lemon peel**, and ½ teaspoon **ground cardamom**. Whirl briefly; stop blender and scrape down sides; whirl until smooth (or combine ingredients in a bowl and beat with rotary mixer until smooth).

Put ¼ cup (⅛ lb.) **butter** or margarine in a 9-inch pie pan; place in preheating oven until butter melts; then remove from oven and pour batter into pan. Bake in a 400° oven until deeply browned and puffy (about 35 minutes); it will be moist in the center. Serve immediately with **Creamy Topping** (directions follow) and **lingonberry preserves** or other tart jam or jelly. Cut in wedges. Makes 6 servings.

Creamy Topping. Beat ½ cup **whipping cream** until stiff. Then gently blend in 3 tablespoons **powdered sugar** and ½ cup **sour cream.** Keep covered and cold if made ahead; blend gently before serving.

Finnish Pancake

(*Suomalainen Pannukakku*)

Almost puddinglike, this hot pancake is a great treat with summer peaches and honey for dessert or breakfast (or use frozen peaches in winter).

- 4 **eggs**
- ¼ cup **honey**
- ¾ teaspoon **salt**
- 2½ cups **milk**
- 1 cup **all-purpose flour, unsifted**
- 4 tablespoons (⅛ lb.) **butter** or margarine
  Sliced peaches
  Honey

Put a 10½-inch oven-proof heavy frying pan or baking pan or dish (at least 3 inches deep) in a 425° oven for about 10 minutes.

Meanwhile, in a bowl beat together eggs, the ¼ cup honey, salt, and milk. Add flour; mix until blended and smooth. Add butter to pan in oven. When butter is melted, pour batter into the hot pan; bake for 25 minutes or until well browned. Serve immediately, cut in wedges and topped with peaches and honey. Makes 4 to 5 main dish servings or 8 to 10 dessert servings.

Fruit Soups, Puddings, and Sauces

Hailing from the days when summer meant more food than you could use at once and winter was a season of limited choice, these recipes present some of the most enduring and well liked fruit creations of Scandinavia.

In summer's brief period of bounty, fruit was, and is, eaten plain just for the joy of having it—or with soft and delicate sauces, such as those in this section, that hide none of the natural flavor. But after the first surge of sampling, the need for variety brought about such refreshing twists as fruit soups—colorful liquids, often with flavors altered or intensified by cooking, to serve at the beginning or end of a meal, or for breakfast. Some may be tempted to call these mixtures compotes or pudding; indeed, the Danes most often do. The title of pudding also bridges the gaps to such other desserts as pear pudding and egg-rich fromages.

Cranberry Fruit Soup

You start with fruit-flavored juice cocktail to make this sparkling soup.

Mix ¾ cup **sugar** with 6 tablespoons **corn starch** in a saucepan. Gradually blend in 3 cups each **cranberry-juice cocktail** and **water.** Add 1 **stick cinnamon**, 2 or 3 inches long, and 2 **whole cloves.** Stirring, bring to a boil, then simmer until clear and slightly thickened. Cover and chill. Serve in individual dishes, topped with **whipped cream** and **sliced almonds.** Makes 12 servings.

Fresh Berry Soup

Make with any tart berry that's in season in your locality, such as boysenberry, raspberry, Olallieberry, or currant. Serve berry soup hot for breakfast or as a first course and chilled for dessert (because as it cools it becomes thicker and more like a pudding).

    1 cup water
       Sugar to taste (about ⅔ cup)
    4 cups fresh cleaned berries
    1½ tablespoons cornstarch
    2 tablespoons water
       Whipping cream, to pour, or
          whipped

In a saucepan bring to a boil 1 cup water combined with the sugar. Add berries and bring to a boil again. Cook for 1 or 2 minutes, taking care that the berries do not overcook and fall apart. Blend cornstarch with 2 tablespoons water and stir into berry mixture. Stirring gently, bring quickly to a boil once more. Serve hot or cold with cream (optional). Makes about 4 servings.

If you don't like berry seeds, force the berry mixture through a wire strainer before adding the cornstarch, but save a few whole uncooked berries for garnish. If you use frozen berries, add no sugar if they are packed in a sugar syrup.

Rhubarb Compote

(*Rabarbergrød*)

Pink and tart, this is a dessert you can also call a compote or a soup. Accompany with cookies.

    1½ pounds rhubarb
    1½ cups water
    1¼ cups sugar
    2 tablespoons cornstarch
       Sweetened whipped cream
    2 tablespoons toasted slivered
          almonds

Finely dice rhubarb. Bring to a full boil with water and sugar, reduce heat, and simmer, uncovered, for 5 to 8 minutes or until rhubarb is very tender. Force through a wire strainer, discarding pulp. You should have about 3½ cups liquid; if not, add water to make this total. Mix about 2 tablespoons of the liquid with cornstarch until smooth; blend into the remaining liquid.

Bring to a boil, stirring constantly, and cook until thickened and clear. Pour into 4 to 6 dessert dishes or a serving bowl and chill until ready to serve. Garnish with puffs of whipped cream and almonds. Makes 4 to 6 servings.

Swedish Fruit Compote

A colorful combination of dried and fresh winter fruits, lightly spiced.

    1 cup sugar
    ¼ cup quick-cooking tapioca
    6 cups water
    2 cups pitted dried prunes
    1 cup dried apricots
    1 cup raisins
    1 cinnamon stick, 3 to 4 inches long
    ¼ teaspoon salt
    3 medium-sized tart apples
    2 or 3 large oranges
       Whipping cream (optional)

Combine in a saucepan the sugar, tapioca, water, prunes, apricots, raisins, cinnamon, and salt. Bring to boiling, stirring until the sugar is dissolved. Lower heat, cover, and simmer gently until the dried fruits are tender but not cooked apart (about 20 minutes). Cool; then chill thoroughly, covered.

Shortly before serving, core and dice or thinly slice the apples (leave the peel on or not, as you prefer). Cut the peel and all the white membrane off the oranges; then slice about ⅛ inch thick, cutting slices in half. Lightly mix in with the other fruits. Serve in a large bowl to ladle into dessert bowls. Offer cream in a pitcher to pour (or whipped cream, if you prefer). Makes about 12 servings.

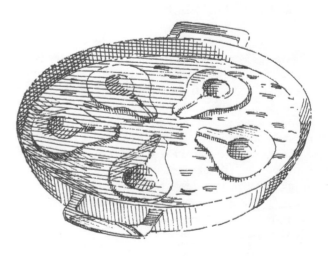

Swedish Pear Pudding

Sugar-glazed pear halves nestle in a soufflélike almond filling for this winter fruit dessert. It can also be made with apples.

3   large firm-ripe Anjou pears or
    Golden Delicious apples
5   tablespoons soft butter or margarine
¾   cup sugar
¼   cup water
⅛   teaspoon ground nutmeg
3   eggs, separated
⅔   cup blanched almonds, toasted
1   cup whipping cream, beaten stiff
    and sweetened

Peel, halve, and core pears or apples. Place in a wide frying pan 2 tablespoons each of the butter and sugar, the water, nutmeg, and halved fruit. Cover and simmer over low heat until tender when pierced (10 to 12 minutes), turning once; set fruit aside. Boil juices until only 3 or 4 tablespoons remain; set aside. Beat egg yolks until thick. Gradually add ½ cup of the sugar, beating until stiff. Grind almonds in a blender (or put through a nut grater) until very fine—the consistency of coarse meal. Mix ground nuts and remaining 3 tablespoons butter into the beaten yolks.

Beat egg whites until soft peaks form; gradually add remaining 2 tablespoons sugar and beat until stiff. Fold meringue into almond mixture. Spoon into a buttered, 10-inch-round baking pan or dish. Arrange pears on top. Bake in a 350° oven for 40 minutes or until set. Serve warm, spooning into individual bowls and topping with whipped cream. Makes about 6 servings.

Citrus Fromage

Fromage, as used in Scandinavia, does not mean cheese (as it does in French). It describes a light and ultra-smooth whipped egg, cream, and gelatin dessert that you can serve from individual dishes or shape in a single, handsome mold.

A fromage makes a fine party dessert, since it must be made ahead in order to chill and set.

To vary flavor and make either lemon or orange fromage, use 1½ teaspoons total of only lemon or orange peel in this dessert.

Mix 1 envelope **unflavored gelatin** with ¾ cup **orange juice** and let stand until softened; then dissolve over hot water.

In the large bowl of a mixer, whip at high speed 3 **eggs** with ⅔ cup **sugar**, 1 teaspoon **grated orange peel**, and ½ teaspoon **grated lemon peel**. When at least double or more in volume, beat in the gelatin mixture and 1 tablespoon **lemon juice**.

With the same unwashed beater, beat 1 cup **whipping cream** until stiff; blend with egg mixture. Pour into 6 to 8 individual dishes. Cover and chill 3 hours or until set. Top with **fresh orange slices,** and, if you like, whole strawberries. Makes 6 to 8 servings.

Molded Citrus Fromage

Follow directions for making **Citrus Fromage** but reduce **orange juice** to ¼ cup. Pour into a fancy 4 to 5-cup mold. Cover and chill at least 6 hours or overnight. To unmold, dip container up to the rim in hot tap water just until edges begin to liquify (takes only a few seconds). Invert a serving dish onto mold, hold together, and turn over. Lift off mold (repeat hot water bath if necessary). Chill briefly to firm surface.

Garnish with the **orange slices, strawberries,** or other berries and **whipped cream.** (You can lightly cover the unmolded dessert and continue to chill until serving time.) Cut or spoon dessert into serving portions. Makes 6 to 8 servings.

Chocolate Fromage

Crunchy bits of semisweet chocolate garnish this smooth dessert. You can flavor the fromage with either cocoa or melted chocolate.

Mix 1 envelope **unflavored gelatin** with ¾ cup cold **water** and let stand until softened; then dissolve over hot water.

In the large bowl of a mixer, whip **3 eggs**, ¾ cup **sugar**, and ¼ cup **cocoa** at high speed until mixture is at least doubled in volume. (Or omit cocoa and melt 4 squares—4 oz.—semisweet chocolate; add to beaten egg.) Beat in gelatin mixture.

With the same unwashed beater, beat 1 cup **whipping cream** until stiff. Stir cream into egg mixture. Pour into 6 to 8 individual dishes. Cover; chill 3 hours or until set.

Coarsely chop or grate about ¼ cup **semisweet chocolate** and sprinkle over desserts. To garnish the fromage in the Danish manner, also top with drained canned **mandarin oranges.** Makes 6 to 8 servings.

Molded Chocolate Fromage

Follow directions for making **Chocolate Fromage** but reduce **water** to ¼ cup. Pour into a fancy 4 to 5-cup mold. Cover and chill at least 6 hours or overnight. To unmold, dip container up to the rim in hot tap water just until edges begin to liquify (takes only a few seconds). Invert a serving dish onto mold, hold together, and turn over. Lift off mold (repeat hot water bath, if necessary). Chill briefly to firm surface. Serve garnished with **whipped cream**; **grated chocolate** and **mandarin oranges** are optional. Makes 6 to 8 servings.

Clabbered Cream

Cooks in Norway use soured cream rather lavishly in cooking and for toppings and sauces, but their cream is smoother and less tart than the sour cream in our markets.

You can duplicate the Norwegian cream at home simply by adding a little buttermilk to cream and letting it stand about a day until clabbered (thickened and smooth but technically curdled). Served plain, or sweetened and flavored; it makes delicious dessert toppings for such dishes as fresh or cooked fruits, fruit pastries, fruit soups, and dessert pancakes.

Unlike commercial sour cream, this cream can be whipped and does not separate when heated.

It keeps several weeks, time enough to try it served and flavored in several ways. Or use it to make Sour Cream Porridge (see below).

In a small saucepan, heat 2 cups **whipping cream** to lukewarm (100° to 105°); remove from heat and stir in 2 tablespoons **buttermilk.** Pour mixture into a glass, stainless steel, or plastic container; cover and let stand at room temperature (65° to 75°) for about 24 hours or until it reaches the consistency of yogurt. Refrigerate, covered, and use within 2 weeks. Serve cold, thick and plain, or stir vigorously to break up curd (making more liquid) and sweeten to taste with **powdered sugar**. Spoon onto any food that is good with whipped cream or sour cream. Makes 2 cups.

Sour Cream Porridge

(*Rommegrøt*)

Rommegrøt is traditionally prepared by the mother of the bride at rural Norwegian wedding feasts. Norwegians also enjoy it topped with blackberry juice and cinnamon-sugar for breakfast, as a dessert, or as a light supper. We suggest serving our version of *rommegrøt* with a small pitcher of melted butter and cinnamon-sugar to sprinkle on top. Or serve it topped with fruit syrup or stewed fruit.

In a small saucepan, combine 2 cups **milk,** 1 cup **Clabbered Cream** (see this **page**), 1 teaspoon **sugar**, and ¼ teaspoon **salt**; bring to a gentle boil. Add 2 tablespoons **farina**, reduce heat to low, and simmer, stirring occasionally, until porridge is smooth and thickened (takes about 15 minutes).

Blend 2 tablespoons **cornstarch** with 2 tablespoons milk to make a smooth paste; gradually stir into the porridge. Continue cooking, stirring constantly, until porridge comes to a boil. Ladle into bowls and serve hot. Add to each portion one or more of these toppings: **melted butter, cinnamon-sugar, fruit syrup,** or **cooked fruit.** Makes about 4 servings.

Swedish Cream

Offer this topping as you would sweetened whipped cream. It is a little less rich.

Beat 1 **egg white** until frothy; then gradually beat in ¾ cup sifted **powdered sugar** and continue to whip until white holds shiny, soft peaks. Set aside. With the same mixer, beat ½ cup **whipping cream** with 1 **egg yolk** until mixture is stiff. Add ½ teaspoon **vanilla** and fold in the beaten egg white. Makes about 1½ cups.

Tools of the Trade

Irons (*l. to r.*) *for waffles, rosettes,* aebleskiver, *pancakes,* krumkake.

Special utensils give some of the pastries in this chapter their proper shape. All the tools are widely available in department store houseware sections, gourmet cookware shops, and through mail order houseware companies. For the most part, they are all modestly priced. (However, when a more commonplace utensil also works, directions are included for its use.)

Krumkake iron. A cooky iron consisting of 2 patterned disks, 5 or 6 inches in diameter, hinged and fitted into a cradle that supports the iron over the heat source. A *krumkake* iron can be used equally well on gas or electric heat. Other cooky irons of similar design—such as the French *gaufrette* iron and Italian *cialde* or *pizzelle* irons—can also be used to make *Krumkake*. Conversely, these other cookies can also be made in the *krumkake* iron. Some of the irons are electrically heated like a waffle iron.

Aebleskiver (or ebleskiver) iron or pan. Shaped much like an inverted frying pan; on the surface are half sphere depressions—usually 7 or more. Use over direct heat to make ball-shaped pancakes.

Swedish pancake pan or platte panna. A flat frying pan with shallow, round depressions on the surface—usually 7 or more—that you fill with a thin batter to make neatly shaped, little round pancakes to serve for dessert or even for breakfast.

Scandinavian or Swedish waffle iron. The waffle grids are a series of hearts joined together; the waffles can be broken apart to make individual hearts. The iron is either electrified or is placed over direct heat (some have cradle supports). Any waffle batter can be baked in it.

Rosette or timbale irons. Used for making fragile fried pastries, rosette irons have fanciful forms, such as flowers, butterflies, stars, and others that create a lacy effect. Timbales are solid forms—rounds, squares, and such, or representational shapes, such as vegetables or trees. The finished pastry forms a cup.

The two kinds of fried pastry irons are used in the same manner. They are screwed onto a metal rod attached to a heat-proof handle; one or two irons may be attached to the same handle. The irons are placed in the cooking oil to heat and then dipped into a thin batter. A light coating of the batter adheres to the iron and is returned to the hot oil and fried until crisp and golden. The procedure is repeated to make each pastry, but once a rhythm is established, the pastries accumulate rapidly.

Cordial Beverages

There is no real season for a cup of warming brew when you consider how it might take the chill from a spring or summer eve or bring a feeling of comfort when held by winter-nipped hands. *Glögg* is the grand Scandinavian answer for such dilemmas. A wine based punch, spiced and often fortified with even stronger liquids, *glögg* comes in as great a variety as do cooks. For occasions where a non-alcoholic beverage is more appropriate, you'll find the one based on cranberry and apple juice suitable for a youthful skating party or a mid-winter child's birthday celebration.

Flaming Glögg

This quickly assembled *glögg* combines wine and several spirits to feed the lively flame. You warm the liquid in the kitchen but bring it out before guests to set afire, ladling the blazing punch over melting sugar cubes.

Inexpensive, dry red wines work well as the base for *glögg;* but for variation, a specific varietal, such as Zinfandel or a Gamay, adds a nice quality.

> 1 bottle (4/5 qt.) dry red wine
> 1 cup dry Sherry
> 1 cup Vodka
> 10 to 15 whole cloves
> 1 cinnamon stick, 2 to 3 inches long
> About ⅔ cup sugar cubes
> About ¾ cup *each* raisins and whole almonds

In an attractive 3-quart saucepan or kettle combine wine, Sherry, vodka, cloves, and cinnamon stick. Place over moderate heat until just hot enough to still sip comfortably; do not boil.

Remove from heat and present for flaming before your guests (do not set pan beneath an exhaust fan or anything that can catch fire). Mound as many sugar cubes as possible in a slotted spoon or ladle and dip quickly into *glögg*. Lift out at once; hold a lighted match close to surface of punch to set aflame. Then spoon *glögg* frequently over cubes to melt sugar and maintain flame (agitating the liquid releases the alcohol fumes that burn). Add any remaining sugar to ladle and melt by the same technique or simply stir into *glögg*.

You can serve the *glögg* as it flames; keep it warm on an electric warming tray or over a candle until all is served. Add a few raisins and almonds to each individual cup. You might offer small spoons for dipping almonds and raisins out of cups to eat after the *glögg* is sipped. Makes 5 cups or 10 servings of ½-cup-sized portions.

Spiced Glögg

Somewhat more subdued and subtle is this version of *glögg*. The spices steep with the wine for several hours or longer, then are removed. The punch is merely warmed (there is not enough alcohol to support a flame).

> 1½ teaspoons whole cardamom seed (pod discarded), slightly crushed
> ½ teaspoon whole cloves
> 1 tablespoon chopped candied ginger
> 4 strips orange peel, ½ inch wide and 2 or 3 inches long, pared thinly with a vegetable peeler
> 2 cinnamon sticks, *each* 2 to 3 inches long
> 1 bottle (4/5 qt.) dry red wine
> ⅓ cup sugar
> ⅔ cup raisins
> About ½ cup whole almonds

In a glass or stainless steel bowl, combine cardamom, cloves, ginger, orange peel, cinnamon, wine, and sugar. Cover and let stand at least 6 hours or overnight. Pour wine through a wire strainer and discard residue. Add raisins to wine and heat just until hot enough to still sip comfortably; do not boil. Keep warm while serving over a candle

or on an electric warming tray. Ladle into cups, getting some of the raisins in each portion. Add a few almonds to each cup as served. Makes 3½ cups or 7 servings of ½-cup-sized portions.

Flaming Apple Punch with Baked Oranges

The whole fruit floats attractively in the punch.

```
6  whole oranges
60 to 72 whole cloves
1  gallon apple juice or cider
3  cinnamon sticks, each 2 or 3 inches
       long
   About 1 cup rum
```

Stud each orange with 10 to 12 cloves. Place oranges slightly apart in a shallow pan. Bake in a 300° oven for 2 hours or until juice begins to drain from oranges. Heat apple cider with oranges (and juice) and cinnamon to simmer in a large kettle (about 8 qt. size). Keep hot to serve on an electric warming tray or over a low flame. Also heat 1 cup rum to warm, ignite, and pour flaming into cider, stirring until flame dies. Add more rum to taste, if desired. Ladle into cups and serve. Makes about 16 cups or 32 servings of ½-cup-sized portions.

Crimson Apple Punch

This makes a pretty beverage for a brunch.

In a large kettle, combine 1 gallon **apple juice** or cider, 2 quarts **cranberry-juice cocktail,** 3 **whole cinnamon sticks** *each* 2 or 3 inches long, and 8 **whole cloves;** heat to simmering. Pour into a large punch bowl or into a kettle that you can keep hot on an electric warming tray or over a low flame. Stir in ¼ cup **lemon juice** and garnish with thin, **unpeeled orange slices.** Makes 1½ gallons or 48 servings of ½-cup-sized portions.

A Ritual of Flames

Welcoming and warming, a cup of *glögg* is a Scandinavian tradition that well suits winter holiday festivities. This hot wine punch, aromatic with spices and with a dramatic blue flame dancing over it, is a cordial way to greet guests for almost any kind of gathering.

You can start with jug or varietal wines. The making of *glögg* (the ö is close to the *ew* in few) is an imaginative procedure. Some families have established a ritual of mellowing the wine with flavorings—for a few hours or up to several days. Others pour the makings into a kettle and heat them together just before serving. Raisins and almonds can go into the *glögg* at any time during its preparation or service. They are chewy treats when cups are emptied; or you can offer spoons before drinking for dipping out these winy treasures.

You can have a dessert party with *glögg*, offering cookies and cake to go with the punch. Particularly pleasant times to serve the drink are to accompany such activities as the decorating of a Christmas tree, filling stockings, or wrapping gifts—or to give to those coming in from the cold after skiing or ice skating.

Ladle Flaming Glögg (see page 77) *over sugar cubes, then into cups; add raisins and almonds.*

Index